A Citizen's Introduction to the Declaration of Independence and the Constitution

A Citizen's Introduction to the Declaration of Independence and the Constitution

By Matthew Spalding, Ph.D.

PREFACE

by Edwin Meese III

The Constitution of the United States has endured for over two centuries. It remains the object of reverence for nearly all Americans and an object of admiration by peoples around the world. William Gladstone was right in 1878 when he described the U.S. Constitution as "the most wonderful work ever struck off at a given time by the brain and purpose of man."

Part of the reason for the Constitution's enduring strength is that it is the complement of the Declaration of Independence. The Declaration provides the philosophical basis for our government and defines the conditions of a free people whose rights and liberty are derived from their Creator. The Constitution delineates the structure of government and the rules for its operation, consistent with the creed of human liberty proclaimed in the Declaration.

The most important themes of the Constitution reflect the mandate of the Declaration of Independence, starting with the recognition that the ultimate authority of a legitimate government depends on the consent of a free people. Thomas Jefferson had set forth the basic principle in his famous formulation:

> We hold these truths to be self-evident, that all men are created equal, that they are endowed by their Creator with certain unalienable Rights, that among these are Life, Liberty, and

> the pursuit of Happiness. That to secure these
> rights, Governments are instituted among Men
> deriving their just powers from the consent of
> the governed.

That "all men are created equal" means that they are equally endowed with unalienable rights. Nature does not single out who is to govern and who is to be governed; there is no divine right of kings. Nor are rights a matter of legal privilege or the benevolence of some ruling class. Fundamental rights exist by nature, prior to government and conventional laws. It is because these individual rights are left unsecured that governments are instituted among men.

Consent is the means by which equality is made politically operable and whereby arbitrary power is thwarted. The natural standard for judging whether a government is legitimate is whether that government rests on the consent of the governed. Any political powers not derived from the consent of the governed are, by the laws of nature, illegitimate and hence unjust.

The "consent of the governed" stands in contrast to "the will of the majority," a view more current in European democracies. The "consent of the governed" describes a situation where the people are self-governing in their communities, religions, and social institutions and into which the government may intrude only with the people's consent. There exists between the people and limited government a vast social space in which men and women, in their individual and corporate capacities, may exercise their self-governing liberty. In Europe, the "will of the majority" signals an idea that all decisions are ultimately political and are routed through the government. Thus, limited government is not just a desirable objective; it is the essential bedrock of the American polity.

At its deepest level, popular government means a structure of government that rests not only on the consent of the governed, but also on a structure of government wherein the views of the people and their civic associations can be expressed and translated into public law and public policy, subject, of course, to the limits established by the Constitution. Through deliberation, debate, and compromise, a public consensus is formed about what constitutes the public good. It is this consensus on fundamental principles that knits individuals into a community of citizens, and it is the liberty to determine the morality of a community that is an important part of our liberty protected by the Constitution.

The Constitution—the original document of 1787 plus its amendments—is and must be understood to be the standard against which all laws, policies, and interpretations should be measured. It is our fundamental law because it represents the settled and deliberate will of the people, against which the actions of government officials must be squared. In the end, the continued success and viability of our democratic Republic depends on our fidelity to, and the faithful exposition and interpretation of, this Constitution, our great charter of liberty.

"If we are to restore America's principles—the truths to which we are dedicated, the common ideas that constitute us as a people—as the central idea of our nation, we must first rediscover them as a people," our author argues. "To do so demands that we rediscover the Declaration of Independence and the U.S. Constitution."

This publication is part of a series of occasional booklets published by The Heritage Foundation, under the auspices of the B. Kenneth Simon Center for American Studies, on the "First Principles" of the American tradition of ordered liberty that we seek to conserve "for ourselves and our posterity," as it says in our Constitution. Other publications cover a range of themes and topics, each aimed at explaining our most primary ideas—which often have been forgotten or rejected—and considering what those principles should mean for America today.

The series is motivated by a powerful observation: Those that lead our nation today—and those who will lead it tomorrow—must *know* and *understand* our first principles if they mean to vindicate those principles and see to it that they once again guide our country. At a time when more and more Americans are searching for a touchstone of principle in the midst of calls for constant political change and the unending expansion of government, this project is more important than ever.

To discuss this topic, we have turned to our own Matthew Spalding, Director of Heritage's B. Kenneth Simon Center for American Studies. The idea of regrounding American politics in the principles of the American Founding—not as historical curiosity but as a source of assurance and guidance for today—is the great theme of his book *We Still Hold These Truths: Rediscovering Our Principles, Reclaiming Our Future.* This monograph is mostly taken from that work, although made more direct and focused in order to create what is needed right now during this teaching moment: *A Citizen's Introduction to the Declaration of Independence and the Constitution.*

Edwin Meese III

Ronald Reagan Distinguished Fellow in Public Policy
and Chairman of the Center for Legal and Judicial Studies

A CITIZEN'S
INTRODUCTION TO THE
DECLARATION OF INDEPENDENCE
AND THE CONSTITUTION

*I*n 1776, when America announced its independence as a nation, it was composed of 13 colonies surrounded by hostile powers.

Today, the United States is a country of 50 states covering a vast continent. Its military forces are the most powerful in the world. Its economy produces almost a quarter of the world's wealth. The American people are among the most hardworking, church-going, affluent, and generous in the world.

What is to account for this monumental success?

Every nation derives meaning and purpose from some unifying quality—an ethnic character, a common religion, a shared history. The United States is different. America was founded at a particular time, by a particular people, on the basis of particular principles about man, liberty, and constitutional government.

The American Revolution drew on old ideas. The United States is the product of Western civilization, shaped by Judeo–Christian culture and the political liberties of Great Britain. Yet the founding of the United States was also *revolutionary*. Not in the sense of replacing one set of rulers with another or overthrowing the institutions of society, but in proclaiming a new basis of political rule in the sovereignty of the people. Indeed, the American Founders constructed their whole organization of government on the capacity of the people to govern themselves.

All of these arguments and then some are to be found in two brief documents. The Declaration of Independence is a timeless statement of inherent rights, the proper purposes of government, and the limits on political authority. Since its ratification in 1789, the United States Constitution has secured our fundamental rights, providing for an unprecedented degree of human freedom and at the same time upholding the rule of law—the framework for the building of a great, prosperous, and just nation unlike any other. To this day, so many years after the American Revolution, the principles proclaimed in the Declaration and promulgated by the Constitution still define us as a nation and inspire us as a people.

If we are to restore America's principles—the truths to which we are dedicated, the common ideas that constitute us as a people—as the central idea of our nation, we must first rediscover them. To do so demands that we rediscover the Declaration of Independence and the U.S. Constitution. We must read them anew and come to understand them as the Founders wrote them and intended them to be understood. Only then can we renew our commitment to them, to the heritage they have given us, and—more important—to the noble ideas and grand promises they contain.[1]

---

[1] This discussion is adapted from Matthew Spalding, *We Still Hold These Truths: Rediscovering Our Principles, Reclaiming Our Future* (Wilmington, Del.: ISI Books, 2009). All the quotes in this monograph can be found in a searchable database at *WeStillHoldTheseTruths.org*.

THE ROAD TO REVOLUTION

The American Revolution began as a tax revolt. The American Revenue Act of 1764 (sometimes called the Sugar Act) expanded various import and export duties, and the first direct tax levied on America was the Stamp Act in 1765. The British ended up repealing the tax, but in the Declaratory Act of 1766, they flatly rejected the Americans' general argument by asserting that Parliament was absolutely sovereign and retained full power to make laws for the colonies "in all cases whatsoever." In 1767, the British government passed a new series of revenue measures (called the Townshend Acts) which placed import duties (external taxes) on a number of essential goods including paper, glass, lead, and tea.

It was at Boston in the spring of 1770 that, tensions running high, British soldiers fired on a large crowd of protesters, wounding 11 colonials and killing five. The Boston Massacre, as it was quickly called, marked the final downturn in the relationship between Britain and the American colonies. By late 1772, Samuel Adams and others were creating new Committees of Correspondence that would link together patriot groups in all 13 colonies and eventually provide the framework for a new government.

In December 1773, a group of colonists disguised as Indians boarded ships of several British merchants and, in protest of British colonial policies, dumped overboard an estimated £10,000 worth of tea in Boston Harbor. "The die is cast," reported John Adams. The British government responded harshly by punishing Massachusetts— closing Boston Harbor, virtually dissolving the Massachusetts Charter, taking control of colonial courts and restricting town meetings, and allowing British troops to be quartered in any home or private building. In response to these "Intolerable Acts," the various Committees of Correspondence banded together and planned an even larger congress of all the colonies to meet in Philadelphia in September 1774.[2]

The First Continental Congress set a clear tone from the start. The Congress set aside a loyalist-proposed reconciliation plan that would have created an American legislative body subject to Parliament and instead unanimously adopted what were called the Suffolk Resolves (proposed by a convention in Suffolk County, Massachusetts), declaring the Intolerable Acts to be "unconstitutional," resolving to boycott British imports, instructing Massachusetts to form a government free of British authority, and calling on the colonies to prepare for the possibility of war.

Delegates also discussed the basis upon which to defend their rights. It was increasingly clear that appeals to common law and charters, to Parliament and to the king, and to the rights of Englishmen were crucially important but ultimately insufficient in defending their liberties. Richard Henry Lee, for instance, observed that the rights of the colonists "are built on a fourfold foundation; on nature, on the British constitution, on charters, and on immemorial usage," but then advocated "lay[ing] our rights upon the broadest bottom, the ground of nature."

In the end, delegates agreed that their strongest case was based on this ground, and that meant making human nature— "a resource to which we might be driven by parliament much sooner than we are aware," noted John Adams—the true foundation for their claims. The classic statement of this argument would be the Declaration of Independence.

The Second Continental Congress convened just one month after fighting had broken out at Lexington and Con-

---

2. The classic work on these British measures and colonial opposition to them is Merrill Jensen's *The Founding of a Nation: A History of the American Revolution 1763–1776* (New York: Oxford University Press, 1968).

cord and only days before the Battle of Bunker Hill. One of its first acts was to recognize the various local militias that had instinctively surrounded the British at Boston as a Continental Army and appoint George Washington of Virginia—the only one among them with any real military experience—as its commander. It also sent to the king one last attempt at reconciliation, called the Olive Branch Petition. To make sure there was no confusion about its absolute seriousness, though, the Congress also issued a "Declaration of the Causes and Necessities for Taking Up Arms," avowing that, if necessary, the colonists were "resolved to die Free men rather than live slaves." King George III refused to receive the colonial petition, issuing instead a Royal Proclamation of Rebellion regarding his disloyal subjects and promising "to bring the Traitors to Justice." The break was now complete and irreparable.

Thomas Paine's *Common Sense* issued the first clarion call in January 1776: "Everything that is right and natural pleads for separation. The blood of the slain, the weeping voice of nature cries, 'TIS TIME TO PART.'" The sentiment for independence was building, and hostilities made the decision all the more imperative.

And so on June 7, 1776, Richard Henry Lee, a delegate from Virginia, proposed a resolution to declare that "these United Colonies are, and of right ought to be, free and independent states," to establish a formal confederation of the colonies and to seek alliances between the united colonies and other nations. Each of these matters was referred to a select committee; the last two would lead to the Articles of Confederation and the Franco–American Treaty of 1778, which was crucial to fighting and winning America's War of Independence.[3]

[3.] Samuel Flagg Bemis's *The Diplomacy of the American Revolution* (New York and London: D. Appleton-Century, 1935) remains the standard work on this aspect of American history.

Congress debated extensively and eventually passed Lee's resolution in favor of independence on July 2, and then it took two more days to debate and amend a committee's draft declaration, approving it on July 4. The separate consideration of Lee's resolution of independence and the committee's language to declare that independence suggests that more was required than a simple announcement of withdrawal from the British Empire. Had that been the objective, Lee's resolution itself would have been sufficient. A "decent respect for the opinions of mankind," however, demanded a broader statement of the principles that justified their actions.

A DECLARATION OF INDEPENDENCE

Although Congress had appointed a distinguished committee to draft the Declaration of Independence—including John Adams, Benjamin Franklin, Roger Sherman, and Robert Livingston—the document is chiefly the work of Thomas Jefferson. Jefferson originally proposed that John Adams draft the Declaration, but Adams made the case to Jefferson that he must be the writer: "Reason first—You are a Virginian, and a Virginian ought to appear at the head of this business. Reason second—I am obnoxious, suspected, and unpopular. You are very much otherwise. Reason third—You can write ten times better than I can."

By his own account, Jefferson was neither aiming at originality nor taking from any particular writings but was expressing what he called the "harmonizing sentiments of the day." The basic theory of the document reflected English Whig thought as it had been developed in the preceding century and a half. By 1776, the ideas of the Declaration—about nature, rights, and government—were well established in the colonies. George Mason had anticipated much of its substance in his draft of the Virginia Declaration of Rights one month earlier.

Jefferson stressed that he had written the Declaration to be "an expression of the American mind" and used language so as to "place before mankind the common sense of the subject, in terms so plain and firm as to command their assent." He did his job well.

The Declaration of Independence is structured in the form of a common-law legal document: preamble, statement of principle, indictment, and conclusion. The stated purpose is to "declare the causes" that impelled the Americans to separate from the British. The document's famous second paragraph is a succinct and powerful synthesis of American constitutional and republican ideas. All these years later, its familiar opening words remain striking:

> We hold these truths to be self-evident, that all men are created equal, that they are endowed by their Creator with certain unalienable Rights, that among these are Life, Liberty and the pursuit of Happiness.—That to secure these rights, Governments are instituted among Men, deriving their just powers from the consent of the governed,—That whenever any Form of Government becomes destructive of these ends, it is the Right of the People to alter or to abolish it, and to institute new Government, laying its foundation on such principles and organizing its powers in such form, as to them shall seem most likely to effect their Safety and Happiness.

The bulk of the document is a bill of indictment accusing King George III of some 30 offenses: some constitutional, some legal, and some matters of policy. In general, these grievances not only track the colonial complaints, but also foreshadow many of the protections included 12 years later in the United States Constitution. A perennial favorite: "He has erected a

7

multitude of New Offices, and sent hither swarms of Officers to harass our People, and eat out their substance." But the key charge was that the king had conspired with Parliament to subject America to a "jurisdiction foreign to our constitution."

At this point in their constitutional development, the Americans argued that a common king with authority over each of the colonies was their only binding legal connection with Great Britain. Parliament was not a party to the various original compacts with the individual colonies and thus could not tax them or regulate their internal affairs. This explains why the colonists' final appeals—and the Declaration of Independence itself—were addressed to the king and not to Parliament. Through his own actions (and inactions) leading up to the American Revolution, intentionally violating those agreements and explicitly placing America outside his protection, George III had himself rebelled, thereby dissolving the colonists' obligations of allegiance.

The combined charges against the king were intended to demonstrate a history of repeated injuries, all having the object of establishing "an absolute tyranny" over the colonies. And while the previously loyal subjects were "disposed to suffer, while Evils are sufferable," the time had come to acknowledge that the relationship had come to an end: "But when a long train of abuses and usurpations, pursuing invariably the same Object, evinces a design to reduce them under absolute Despotism, it is their right, it is their duty, to throw off such Government."

ARE ALL MEN CREATED EQUAL?

So what did the Continental Congress mean in asserting— going so far as to say it is "self-evident"—that all men are *equal?* This seems to make no sense. Ordinary experience tells us the exact opposite: There are innumerable differences—in size, shape, color, intelligence, you name it—and no two individuals are exactly alike. But these kinds of differences are not what Jefferson (or the Continental Congress that approved the Declaration) had in mind. Let us try to understand the matter as they understood it.

The Declaration of Independence makes its claim for American independence based on "the Laws of Nature and of Nature's God." In looking to nature, the Founders did not mean the outdoors—the trees, lakes, and animals that make up the natural environment. They meant nature as in the design or purpose of things, as birds by nature fly just as fish by nature swim. Different things have different natures.

Man has a distinguishing nature as well; it has to do with distinctive capacities and characteristics. Other species follow instinct and, as a result, are not responsible for their actions. Wolves, for instance, cannot be said to be responsible for killing sheep: That's what wolves do. But human beings are different: They are capable of imagination, deliberation, judgment, and choice in their actions and so can be held morally accountable. It is this ability to contemplate right and wrong and to act accordingly that distinguishes men from other animals. In this sense, man is by nature unique among animals and alone has the capacity for liberty.

That "all men" are created equal is not a reference to males as opposed to females; it means the whole human species. Indeed, the observed inequalities of individual men and women (such as size, shape, and color) are insignificant and dramatically underscore the ways in which all human beings, as a species, are equal in their nature.[4]

[4.] Hadley Arkes's *First Things: An Inquiry into the First Principles of Morals and Justice* (Princeton, N.J.: Princeton University Press, 1986) investigates this concept in greater depth.

It says in the Declaration of Independence that this equality is "self-evident." In what sense? To say that something is self-evident does not mean that it is *obvious*; it means that something is evident in itself once one understands the terms involved. Once we understand that "man" has a certain nature, for instance, it becomes self-evident that all men, by sharing the same nature, are equal. We can understand this to be "self-evident" regardless of whether we believe nature to have been created (as in "all men are *created* equal") or observed by reason, as in the language of the Virginia Declaration of Rights ("all men are by nature equally free and independent").

THE LAWS OF NATURE AND NATURE'S GOD

This understanding of human nature reaches back to both classical philosophy and biblical theology—as in "the Laws of Nature" as well as "nature's God"—and represents a profound agreement between reason and revelation about man and the proper ground of politics. The Founders understood the argument for natural rights to be a continuation of both the English republican tradition—in writers such as John Locke and Algernon Sidney, whose works were widely read and admired in America—and a natural law tradition dating back to medieval thinkers such as Thomas Aquinas and further to classical thinkers such as Aristotle and Cicero. The "harmonizing sentiments" expressed in the Declaration of Independence, Jefferson wrote, could be found in conversation, letters, essays, and "the elementary books of public right, as Aristotle, Cicero, Locke, Sidney, etc." One can also see these arguments woven together in religious sermons of the day, associating human nature and natural rights with theological views of creation and moral obligation, pointing out that God created man and is the author of the laws of nature.

Because of this nature, each man is his own natural ruler, with the capacity to govern himself. Unlike an animal, man can make decisions about how to live his own life and conduct his affairs. Because man is rational and seeks relationships with others to fulfill that nature, men can live in communities based on agreed purposes and common understandings of justice.

At the same time, man is a bundle of desires and emotions and is prone to allow his passions to overrule his reason. It is with this inclination in mind that Madison famously wrote in *Federalist* 10 that "the latent causes of faction are sown in the nature of man." And recall his memorable observation from *Federalist* 51: "It may be a reflection on human nature, that such devices should be necessary to control the abuses of government. But what is government itself, but the greatest of all reflections on human nature? If men were angels, no government would be necessary."

The Founders' view of nature was by no means wholly negative. "As there is a degree of depravity in mankind which requires a certain degree of circumspection and distrust," Madison observed in *Federalist* 55, "so there are other qualities in human nature which justify a certain portion of esteem and confidence." The choosing of moral actions shapes habits and gives rise to virtue. But it was a sober view, consistent with classical philosophy as well as the Christian concept of man fallen from divine grace. The givens of human nature—the highs, the lows, and the in-betweens—had to be accounted for in forming government, and its weaknesses had to be moderated and corrected by moral education and character formation.

The emphasis on nature is profoundly significant, as it provided the philosophical mooring for everything else.[5] It was

---

5.   On the importance of foundational concepts in American political thought, see James Ceaser's *Nature and History in American Political Development: A Debate* (Cambridge, Mass.: Harvard University Press, 2006).

the concept that defined the grounds and legitimate ends of politics and political community. As such, it is the necessary premise of the foundational and operational first principles of American liberty.

EQUAL NATURAL RIGHTS

The idea of grounding the first principles of liberty in the equal human nature of all persons has great implications. The natural relationship between man and horse, for instance, is that of master and servant because, in the order of nature, man is rationally superior to beast. But no such relationship exists, by nature, between man and man. Jefferson once described this relationship using a powerful analogy from Algernon Sidney: "[T]he mass of mankind has not been born with saddles on their backs, nor a favored few booted and spurred, ready to ride them legitimately, by the grace of God."

That man is unique in the scheme of creation also means that man is entitled to certain rights that result from that common humanity.[6] A right is something that justly belongs to someone and creates a claim against those who deprive one of that right. One person's right implies an equivalent duty in others not to interfere unjustly with that right. In terms of these fundamental rights (called "natural rights"), we are all equal—no one has more and no one less—and equally free.

While there are, of course, dramatic differences in abilities and talents, all persons are equal before the law and are to be given equal protection of the same fundamental rights. John Adams articulated this case in his *Discourses on Davila* when he wrote that:

[6.] On the unique American understanding of rights, see Charles Kesler, "The Nature of Rights in American Politics: A Comparison of Three Revolutions," Heritage Foundation *First Principles Essay* No. 18, September 30, 2008.

[A]mong men, all are subject by nature to equal laws of morality, and in society have a right to equal laws for their government, yet no two men are perfectly equal in person, property, understanding, activity, and virtue—or ever can be made so by any power less than that which created them.

Two things should be noted in this context.

First, it is important to understand that the philosophical grounding in natural rights does not create a radical and unlimited sense of freedom, as some claim today. The argument of the American Founders is of rights derived from a human nature understood in accord with the classical or traditional view of man. The Declaration of Independence says that "all men are created equal and endowed by their creator with *certain* unalienable rights." These are the truly fundamental things, not just anything or everything that we want or claim.

Second, these rights are not the creation or indulgence of government. While additional positive or civil rights (more correctly termed civil liberties) are enshrined in the Constitution—like the rights of free speech and freedom of the press recognized in the Bill of Rights—and Congress can legislatively create "civil" rights, natural rights preexist the institution of government, precisely because they arise out of the natural equality that is the essence of human liberty. Congress (or, more likely today, the courts) cannot just make up rights as it sees fit. Nor can these rights be taken away: They are "unalienable" and cannot be given over (alienated) to someone else.

In the end, it is this sense of rights that ultimately limits government. The law of nature, as Hamilton explained, is "an eternal and immutable law, which is indispensably obligatory upon all mankind, prior to any human institution whatever." Jefferson was more to the point when he wrote that the colonists claimed "their rights as derived from the laws of nature, and not as the gift of their Chief Magistrate."

THE CONSENT OF THE GOVERNED

The consent of the governed follows from man's natural equality and equal rights. If we are all equal and no one (king, a ruling class, intellectual elites) possesses a right to rule by nature, then we must proceed in a way that gives everyone, as much as possible, an equal say in how political rule is formed and operates. Because of our status as equals, it is also the case that legitimate government—that is, government that respects that fundamental equality—must be based on common agreement or consent.

Americans understood government not as a relationship between the ruler and the ruled, but as a voluntary agreement among the sovereign people about how they shall govern themselves to secure the rights they possessed by nature. This was referred to as the "social compact." The idea was espoused by (and came to Americans through the writings of) John Locke and others. Americans saw much of their own history in terms of contract and compact, from the religious view of covenant theology applied in the context of political governance to the fact that individual colonies began with charters between the king and the colonies. For well over a century, Americans developed and became accustomed to the idea of government as having been created through fundamental agreement authorized by popular consent.

The concept can be seen in the Massachusetts Constitution of 1780, which declares: "The body politic is formed by a voluntary association of individuals; it is a social compact by which the whole people covenants with each citizen and each citizen with the whole people." But it is summarized very simply in the words of the Declaration of Independence, which posits as a self-evident truth "that to secure these rights, Governments are instituted among Men, deriving their just powers from the consent of the governed."

In addition to the formation of government in the first place, consent also gives guidance concerning the processes by which legitimate government operates. Among the charges lodged against the king in the Declaration of Independence is that he assented to Parliament's "imposing Taxes on us without our Consent" and "has kept among us, in times of peace, Standing Armies without the Consent of our legislatures." Indeed, the first six charges against the king address interference with local legislation and legislatures, violating "the right of Representation in the Legislature, a right inestimable to them and formidable to tyrants only."

Consent does not necessarily mean pure democratic rule, but it does require some sort of process of popular agreement to lawmaking and governance. In America, this was understood to mean a popular form of representative government. Only a government that derived its power from "the great body of the people," according to *Federalist* 39, was compatible with the "genius of the American people," "the fundamental principles of the revolution," and a determination to "rest all our political experiments on the capacity of mankind for self-government."

On the other hand, consent does not mean mere majoritarianism—that anything and everything the majority demands is right. Lawmaking by consent is not the simple translating of majority will into public policy; it is the product of settled public reasoning consistent with a proper understanding of the first principles of liberty. Consent is the legitimate or just means for securing equal rights, but in the end it remains the *means* rather than the *end* of democratic government.

THE SIGNIFICANCE OF THE DECLARATION

As a practical matter, the Declaration of Independence announced to the world the unanimous decision of the 13 American colonies to separate themselves from Great Britain, but its greatest significance—then as well as now—is its enduring statement of the limits of political authority and the proper ends of government and its proclamation of a new basis of political rule in the sovereignty of the people. The Americans' final appeal was not to any positive law or evolving theory but to rights inherently possessed by all men and "the separate and equal station to which the Laws of Nature and Nature's God" entitled them as a people.

The Declaration of Independence is revolutionary not because a particular group of Americans declared their independence under particular circumstances, but because they did so by appealing to—and promising to base their particular government on—a universal and permanent standard of justice. As such, the Declaration's meaning transcends history and the particulars of the time. Self-evident truths are not restricted to any one era or nation; they are as true today as they were in 1776. It is in this sense that Abraham Lincoln in 1859 praised the author of the Declaration as:

> the man who, in the concrete pressure of a struggle for national independence by a single people, had the coolness, forecast, and capacity to introduce into a merely revolutionary document, an abstract truth, applicable to all men and all times, and so to embalm it there, that to-day, and in all coming days, it shall be a rebuke and a stumbling-block to the very harbingers of re-appearing tyranny and oppression.

THE ROAD TO PHILADELPHIA

In 1774, after Parliament had shut down the Massachusetts legislature and closed the port of Boston, the First Continental Congress advised Massachusetts to form an independent colonial government. In May 1776, a year after the beginning of hostilities at Lexington and Concord, the Second Continental Congress charged the colonies to develop "such Government as shall, in the opinion of the Representatives of the People, best conduce to the happiness and safety of their Constituents in particular, and America in general." These steps led to the development of state constitutions for many of the colonies. The oldest written constitution in the world is the one John Adams wrote for Massachusetts in 1780.

Roundly skeptical of monarchs and overbearing leaders, the new state constitutions increased the power of the legislature to the diminishment of the executive. Most state legislatures appointed the governor and largely excluded him from the legislative process. As well, most state constitutions gave the governor minimal veto powers and negligible appointive authority and limited his term of office to one year.

At the same time, the colonies together began the process of creating the first constitution of the United States. In resolving to declare American independence in July 1776, the Second Continental Congress called for the drafting of a plan to unify the colonies as a confederation.

Proposed in 1777 and ratified in 1781, the Articles of Confederation are an important bridge between the government of the Continental Congress and that of the current United States Constitution. The experience of the Articles—during which the nation won the Revolutionary War, formed diplomatic relations with major nations around the world, settled land claims, and began western expansion through the Northwest Ordinance while every state remained in the union—was very instructive for the nation.

There had been attempts at national union, the most serious of which was Benjamin Franklin's Albany Plan in 1754, which proposed a governing body and an independent executive for the purposes of handling defense, trade, and the western lands. But with the coming of independence and the exigencies of war, there was a new urgency to regularize the common identity of the colonies.

Because of the colonies' trepidation with respect to British central authority, and based on their successful experience as united colonies, the Articles created a "Confederation and perpetual union" of sovereign states: "Each state retains its sovereignty, freedom and independence, and every power, jurisdiction, and right, which is not by this Confederation expressly delegated to the United States, in Congress assembled." On paper, Congress had the power to make war and peace, regulate coinage, create a postal service, borrow money, and establish uniform weights and measures. From its inception, however, the inherent weaknesses of the Articles of Confederation made it awkward and, finally, unworkable.

Congress under the Articles lacked authority to impose taxes to cover national expenses or enforce requests on the states, and there was no independent executive or judiciary. That is, there was no power to enforce Congress's actions, whether against states or against individuals. Because all 13 states had to ratify amendments, one state's refusal prevented structural reform; nine of 13 states had to approve important legislation, which meant that five states could thwart any major proposal, and although the Confederation Congress could negotiate treaties with foreign powers, all treaties had to be ratified by the states.

By the end of the war in 1783, it was clear that the new system had become, as George Washington observed, "a shadow without the substance." Weakness in international affairs and in the face of continuing European threats in North America, the inability to enforce a peace treaty with Great Britain, and the failure to collect enough taxes to pay foreign creditors all intensified the drive for a stronger national government.[7]

An immediate impetus to re-evaluate the Articles was an armed revolt in 1786–87 called Shays's Rebellion. A group of farmers, objecting to a Massachusetts law requiring that debts be paid in specie and to increasing farm and home foreclosures resulting from the law, took up arms in protest and attacked a federal armory in Springfield, Massachusetts. The rebellion was put down eventually by local militia, but the federal government had been helpless in defending itself or quelling the uprising.

In 1785, representatives from Maryland and Virginia, meeting at George Washington's Mount Vernon home to discuss interstate trade, requested a meeting of the states to discuss trade and commerce. The next year, delegates from several states gathered at a conference in Annapolis, Maryland, to discuss commercial issues. James Madison and Alexander Hamilton persuaded that conference to issue a call for a general convention of all the states "to render the constitution of government adequate to the exigencies of the union," in the convention's words. From May 25 to September 17, 1787, delegates met at Philadelphia in the same statehouse from which

---

[7.]   The classic work on this period is John Fiske's *The Critical Period of American History 1783–1789* (Boston and New York: Houghton, Mifflin, 1888), but a more popular and recent work is *The Perils of Peace: America's Struggle for Survival After Yorktown* (New York: HarperCollins, 2007) by Thomas Fleming.

the Second Continental Congress issued the Declaration of Independence—now called Independence Hall.[8]

THE CONSTITUTIONAL CONVENTION

The Constitutional Convention was one of the most remarkable bodies ever assembled. There were not only leaders in the fight for independence, such as Roger Sherman and John Dickinson, and leading thinkers just coming into prominence, such as James Madison, Alexander Hamilton, and Gouverneur Morris, but also legendary figures, such as Benjamin Franklin and George Washington. Every state was represented, except for Rhode Island, which, fearful that a stronger national government would injure its lucrative trade, opposed any major change in the Articles of Confederation. Patrick Henry and Samuel Adams, both of whom considered a strong national government antithetical to republican principles, also did not attend the convention.

Notably absent were John Jay, who was then the Secretary of Foreign Affairs, and John Adams and Thomas Jefferson, who were both out of the country representing the new nation. Their absence was almost assuredly providential. The attendance of both strong-willed figures might have made it impossible for the convention to make the compromises that proved essential to completion of their work. Nevertheless, Jefferson later described the convention as "an assembly of demigods."

As their first order of business, the delegates unanimously chose Washington as president of the convention. Though he

---

[8]   Clinton Rossiter's *1787: The Grand Convention* (New York: Macmillan, 1966) is very readable and comprehensive, while Catherine Drinker Bowen's *Miracle at Philadelphia: The Story of the Constitutional Convention, May to September 1787* (Boston: Little, Brown, 1966) is more popular and narrative. A more recent work is *The Summer of 1787: The Men Who Invented the Constitution* (New York: Simon & Schuster, 2007) by David O. Stewart.

had initially been hesitant to attend the convention, Washington pushed the delegates to adopt "no temporizing expedient" and instead to "probe the defects of the Constitution [i.e., the Articles of Confederation] to the bottom, and provide radical cures."

While they waited in Philadelphia for a quorum, Washington presided over daily meetings of the Virginia delegation to consider strategy and the set of reform proposals that would become the plan presented at the outset of the convention. Although he contributed to formal debate only once, at the end of the convention, Washington was actively involved throughout the three-and-a-half-month proceedings. "Let us raise a standard to which the wise and honest can repair," he said in his opening remarks. "The event is in the hand of God."

The convention had three basic rules: Voting was to be by state, with each state, regardless of size or population, having one vote; proper decorum was to be maintained at all times; and the proceedings were to be strictly secret. To encourage free and open discussion and debate, the convention shifted back and forth between full sessions and meetings of the Committee of the Whole, a parliamentary procedure that allowed informal debate and flexibility in deciding and reconsidering individual issues. Although the convention hired a secretary, the best records of the debate—and thus the most immediate source of their intentions—are the detailed notes written by James Madison, which, in keeping with the pledge of secrecy, were not published until 1840.[9]

As soon as the convention agreed on its rules, Edmund Randolph, on behalf of the Virginia delegation, presented a

---

[9.] *The Records of the Federal Convention of 1787* (New Haven and London: Yale University Pres, 1986), edited by Max Farrand, gathers into three volumes all the records written by participants of the Constitutional Convention, including the extensive notes taken throughout by James Madison.

set of 15 resolutions, known as the Virginia Plan, which set aside the Articles of Confederation and created a new national government with separate legislative, executive, and judicial branches. This was largely the work of the brilliant young James Madison, who came to the convention extensively prepared and well-versed in the ancient and modern history of republican government. (He prepared a memorandum on the "Vices of the Political System of the United States.") The delegates generally agreed on the powers that should be lodged in a national bicameral legislature but disagreed on how the states and popular opinion should be reflected in it. Under the Virginia Plan, population would determine representation in both houses of Congress, giving the advantage to larger, more populous states.

To protect their equal standing, delegates from less-populous states rallied around William Paterson's alternative New Jersey Plan to amend the Articles of Confederation, which would preserve each state's equal vote in a one-house Congress with slightly augmented powers. When the delegates rejected the New Jersey Plan, Roger Sherman proffered what is often called "the Great Compromise" (or the Connecticut Compromise, after Sherman's home state), under which a House of Representatives would be apportioned based on population and each state would have an equal vote in a Senate. A special Committee of Eleven (one delegate from each state present at the time) elaborated on the proposal, and the convention then adopted it. As a precaution against having to assume the financial burdens of the smaller states, the larger states exacted an agreement that revenue bills could originate only in the House, where the more populous states would have greater representation.

In late July, a Committee of Detail (John Rutledge of South Carolina, Edmund Randolph of Virginia, Nathaniel Gorham of Massachusetts, Oliver Ellsworth of Connecticut, and James Wilson of Pennsylvania) reworked the resolutions of the amended Virginia Plan into a draft constitution. The text now included a list of the key powers of Congress, a "necessary and proper" clause, and a number of prohibitions on the states. Over most of August and into early September, the convention carefully worked over this draft and then gave it to a Committee of Style (William Johnson of Connecticut, Alexander Hamilton of New York, Gouverneur Morris of Pennsylvania, James Madison of Virginia, and Rufus King of Massachusetts) to polish the language.

The literary quality of the Constitution, most prominently the language of the preamble, is due to Morris's work. The delegates continued revising the final draft until September 17 (now celebrated as Constitution Day), when they signed the Constitution and sent it to the Congress of the Confederation, and the convention officially adjourned.

THE RATIFICATION DEBATE

Some of the original 55 delegates had returned home over the course of the summer and were not present at the convention's conclusion. Of the 41 that remained, only three delegates—Edmund Randolph and George Mason of Virginia and Elbridge Gerry of Massachusetts—opposed the Constitution in its completed form and chose not to sign. Randolph, who had introduced the Virginia Plan, thought in the end that the Constitution was not sufficiently republican and was wary of its single executive. Mason and Gerry, who later supported the Constitution and served in the First Congress, were concerned about the lack of a declaration of specific rights. Despite these objections, George Washington thought that it was "little short of a miracle" that the delegates had agreed on a new constitution.

The Philadelphia convention understood in a profound way that the Constitution needed to be a sovereign act of the whole people, not just of state governments. For this reason, on September 28, according to the rules of the Constitution, Congress sent the document to the states to be ratified not by state legislatures but by conventions that were elected by the people of each state.

Those who had concluded that the government under the Articles of Confederation was weak and ineffective, advocated a convention to substantially rework the national government structure, and then supported the new constitution were called "Federalists," while those who opposed changing that structure and then opposed the ratification of the new constitution became known as "Anti-Federalists." Made up of diverse elements and various individuals, the Anti-Federalists initially wrote their criticisms under pseudonyms like "Brutus" (believed to be Robert Yates of New York), "Centinel" (believed to be Samuel Bryan of Pennsylvania), and "Federal Farmer" (the authorship of which is disputed) but found public voice when important revolutionary figures like Patrick Henry came out against the Constitution.

The Anti-Federalists held that the only way to have limited government and self-reliant citizens was through a small republic, and they believed that the Constitution gave too much power to the federal government relative to the states. They were especially suspicious of executive power, fearing that the presidency would devolve into a monarchy over time. At the same time, they warned of judicial tyranny stemming from the creation of independent, life-tenured judges.

While the Anti-Federalists failed to prevent ratification of the Constitution, their efforts, which came to focus on a lack of a federal bill of rights as existed in most state constitutions, led directly to the creation of the first amendments to the U.S. Constitution. Many of their concerns and warnings, whether or not they justified opposition to the Constitution, were prescient in light of modern changes in American constitutionalism.

During the ratification debate in the State of New York, Hamilton, Madison, and John Jay wrote a series of brilliant newspaper essays under the pen name of Publius (a figure from Roman republican history) to refute the arguments of the Anti-Federalists. The 85 essays, mostly published between October 1787 and August 1788, were later collected in book form as *The Federalist*.[10] The initial essays (Nos. 2 through 14) stress the weaknesses of the Confederation and the advantages of a strong and permanent national union. The middle essays (Nos. 15 through 36) argue for energetic government, in particular the need for the government to be able to tax and provide for national defense. The last essays (Nos. 37 through 84) describe the branches and powers of the new government and explain the "conformity of the proposed Constitution to the true principles of republican government."

In recommending *The Federalist*, George Washington wrote that its authors "have thrown a new light upon the science of government, they have given the rights of man a full and fair discussion, and explained them in so clear and forcible a manner, as cannot fail to make a lasting impression." Thomas Jefferson claimed the work was simply "the best commentary on the principles of government which ever was written."[11]

[10.] See *How to Read* The Federalist Papers (Washington: The Heritage Foundation, 2010) by Anthony A. Peacock.

[11.] Of the many editions of *The Federalist Papers*, the Signet Classics edition (New York, 2003), edited by the late Clinton Rossiter and updated with an extended introduction and notes by Charles Kesler, is best. A good collection of essays on *The Federalist* is *Saving the Revolution: The Federalist Papers and the American Founding* (New York: Free Press, 1987), edited by Kesler.

The first state convention to ratify the Constitution was Delaware's, on December 7, 1787; the last convention of the 13 original colonies was that of Rhode Island, on May 29, 1790, two-and-a-half years later. Although there was strong opposition in such states as Massachusetts, Virginia, New York, and North Carolina, in the end, no state convention decided against ratifying the new constitution. During the debates, however, the Anti-Federalists strenuously argued for, and the Federalists agreed to add to the Constitution, a Bill of Rights (to be discussed later). With the ratification by the ninth state convention—New Hampshire, on June 21, 1788—Congress passed a resolution to make the new constitution operative and set dates for choosing presidential electors and the opening session of the new Congress.

READING THE CONSTITUTION

The Constitution begins with a preamble, or introductory clause, that asserts at the very start the authority—"We the People"—that establishes the document and "ordains" or orders it into effect. This is very different from the opening of the Articles of Confederation, which speaks in the name of individual states, and represents an important shift (hotly opposed by the Anti-Federalists) in the understanding of the constitutional sovereignty underlying the document. The Constitution then proclaims the broad objectives of "We the People," their reasons for constituting a new government, and the ends or purposes for which the Constitution is formed.

Of these six reasons, two are immediate requirements of safety and security common to every sovereign nation—"insure domestic tranquility" and "provide for the common defense"—and two look forward to building a particular society that upholds the rule of law and fosters prosperity and well-being for all of its citizens—"establish Justice" and "promote the General Welfare." The other two objectives grandly express the Founders' hopes for their nation's and their people's future: The Constitution is meant to "form a *more perfect* union" and "secure the blessings of liberty to ourselves *and our posterity*."

This statement of purpose is as true and valid today as it was in 1787. If it were not, the remainder of the Constitution would be obsolete and mostly irrelevant.

After the preamble, the rest of the Constitution—being a practical document to create a framework of law—describes the powers, procedures, and institutions of government. This is as it should be. "It is a melancholy reflection that liberty should be equally exposed to danger whether the government have too much power or too little power," Madison observed in a letter to Jefferson, "and that the line which divides these extremes should be so inaccurately defined by experience." Liberty is assured not by the anarchy of no government on the one hand or the arbitrary rule of unlimited government on the other, but through a carefully designed and maintained structure of limited constitutional government.

The Constitution is divided into seven parts, or articles, each dealing with a general subject. Each article is further divided into sections and clauses. The first three articles create three distinct branches of government: the legislature, the executive, and the judiciary. The very form of the document separates the branches in accordance with distinct powers, duties, and responsibilities stemming from the primary functions of governing: to make laws, to execute and enforce the laws, and to uphold (judge or adjudicate) the rule of those laws by applying them to particular individuals or cases.[12]

---

12.   For a clause-by-clause analysis of the document, see *The Heritage Guide to the Constitution* (Washington: The Heritage Foundation, 2005), edited by David Forte and Matthew Spalding.

The Constitution creates three branches of government of equal "rank" in relation to each other. No branch is higher or lower than any other, and no branch controls the others; each has independent authority and unique powers. The order—legislature, executive, judiciary—is important, however, moving from the most to the least "democratic" (that is, from the most to the least directly chosen by the people).

The legislative branch is the first among equals. Its members "are distributed and dwell among the people at large," wrote Madison in *Federalist* 50. "Their connections of blood, of friendship, and of acquaintance embrace a great proportion of the most influential part of the society." As a result, Members of Congress are "more immediately the confidential guardians of their rights and liberties." The Constitution lodges the basic power of government in the legislature not only because it is the branch most directly representative of popular opinion (being the closest to the people), but also because the very essence of governing according to the rule of law is centered on the legitimate authority to make laws.

The Constitution, by its language and nature as a written framework of government, creates a government of *delegated* and *enumerated* powers. Despite the popular term "states' rights," no government (federal, state, county, or local) actually possesses any *rights* at all.

Recall from the Declaration of Independence that *persons* are endowed with unalienable rights. Governments possess only *powers*, which in legitimate governments are derived from the consent of the governed. In particular, governments have only those powers that are given (or delegated) to them by the people. Individuals, who possess rights by nature, hold those powers and may grant some of them to the government. This point is implicit throughout the Constitution but was later stated explicitly in the Tenth Amendment: "The powers not delegated to the United States by the Constitution, nor prohibited by it to the States, are reserved to the States respectively, or to the people."

The concept of enumerated (or listed) powers follows from the concept of delegated powers, as the functional purpose of a constitution is to write down and assign the powers granted to government. The delegation of powers to government and a written agreement as to the extent (and limits) of those powers are critical (if not necessary) elements of limited constitutional government. The scope of government is determined by the extent of power delegated and then enumerated in the Constitution. As we shall see, this enumeration applies especially to the powers delegated to Congress.

In many ways, both minor and fundamental, the Constitution does not operate as it was intended and as it did operate for much of our history. There is a vast disjunction between the Founders' Constitution and the "living" Constitution that is today virtually a dead letter. But before we consider those changes, we must first understand the design and form of the original constitutional order.

ARTICLE I: THE LEGISLATIVE POWER

Each of the first three articles opens with what is called a "vesting clause" that describes the unique powers vested in, or entrusted to, each particular branch of government. The Constitution does not grant any power to the federal government; it grants power only to the institutions created in the three branches of the government. As a result, the differing language of these clauses in each article is very important.

Article I begins: "All legislative powers herein granted shall be vested in a Congress of the United States, which shall consist of a Senate and House of Representatives." This language implies that while there might be other legislative powers, Congress is granted only those "herein" granted, meaning listed in various clauses of the Constitution.

The legislative power extends to 17 topics listed in Article I, Section 8: taxing and borrowing, interstate and foreign commerce, naturalization and bankruptcy, currency and counterfeiting, post offices and post roads, patents and copyrights, federal courts, piracy, the military, and the governance of the national capitol and certain federal enclaves. All told, the powers are not extensive, but they are vital. Apart from some relatively minor matters, the Constitution added to the authority already granted in the Articles of Confederation only the powers to regulate foreign and interstate commerce and to apportion "direct" taxes among the states according to population.

The diverse powers granted to Congress might at first seem rather disorganized, ranging from the clearly momentous (to declare war) to the seemingly minute (to fix weights and measures); but upon reflection, an underlying pattern emerges based on the distinction between key functions assigned to the national government and those left to the state governments. The two most important functions concern the nation's security (such as the powers to maintain national defense) and the national economy (such as the power to tax or to regulate interstate commerce).

As might be expected, many of the powers complement each other in supporting those functions: The power to regulate interstate commerce, for instance, is consistent with the power to control currency, which is supported in turn by the power to punish counterfeiting and to establish standards for weights and measures. How can an economy function without a common currency?

While the federal government's powers are *limited*, the powers granted are *complete*. The objective was to create an energetic government that could effectively accomplish its purposes. The federal government must have all powers needed to do the jobs assigned to it. As such, the granted powers are supported by the auxiliary authority needed to carry out these functions.

The central example of this is what is called the "necessary and proper" clause, which empowers Congress to "make all Laws which shall be necessary and proper for carrying into Execution the foregoing Powers, and all other Powers vested by this Constitution in the Government of the United States, or in any Department or Officer thereof." While this language suggests a wide sweep of "implied" powers, it is not a grant to do anything and everything, but only to make those additional laws that are necessary and proper for execution of the powers expressed in the Constitution. Jefferson read this clause extremely narrowly, and Hamilton read it too broadly. Madison expressed the more balanced view, writing that a necessary and proper law requires "a definite connection between means and ends," in which those means and ends are linked "by some obvious and precise affinity."

"It neither enlarges any power specifically granted; nor is it a grant of any new power to Congress," wrote Joseph Story in his *Commentaries on the Constitution*. "But it is merely a declaration for the removal of all uncertainty, that the means of carrying into execution those, otherwise granted, are included in the grant." While the exact limits of the necessary and proper clause have always been debated, the provision clearly allows Congress to adapt its stated powers to the various crises of the times so that the Constitution can endure. "This provision is made in a Constitution intended to endure for ages to come," John Marshall wrote in *Marbury v. Madison*, "and consequently to be adapted to the various crises of human affairs."

The point is clear: Congress has only the powers delegated to it in the Constitution. The legislature holds the primary position in republican government, being responsible for the core lawmaking function and thus most of the activities of government. As the legislature is also the most popular branch of government—and so the most prone to the temporary passions and narrow interests of democratic majorities—its power must be especially bounded. If Congress could do whatever it wanted, Madison noted in a 1792 letter, then the government is "no longer a limited one, possessing enumerated powers, but an indefinite one, subject to particular exceptions."

To further limit the expansion of legislative power and control the legislative branch in relation to the rest of the government, Article I divides Congress into two chambers (bicameralism) chosen by two different political constituencies and with different terms of office: the House of Representatives, each member being elected by districts every two years, and the Senate, with members originally appointed by state legislatures to serve staggered terms of six years each. The House is based on popular representation, and the Senate is based on equal representation of all of the states.

Unlike the House, which is intended to be responsive to the ebb and flow of popular opinion, the Senate—with its longer terms of office and a larger and distinct constituency—was to be more stable, deliberative, and oriented toward long-term state and national concerns. It is because of the nature of the Senate that the chamber is given unique responsibilities concerning the approval of executive appointments (judges, ambassadors, and all other officers of the United States) and treaties with other countries.

ARTICLE II: THE EXECUTIVE POWER

What to do with executive power proved to be more difficult. The primary reason, of course, was that Americans had fought a revolution to escape monarchical rule. Through "repeated injuries and usurpations," as it says in the Declaration of Independence, the king of England proved that he was "unfit to be the ruler of a free people." By the time of the Constitutional Convention in 1787, most delegates had become convinced that a strong national executive was necessary, but they nevertheless remained extremely wary of the dangers (and tendencies) of executive tyranny. Tyranny by executives, whether Caesars, kings, or military dictators, had been a problem throughout history.

Ultimately, the Constitutional Convention was confident in the creation of the presidency because of the widespread assumption that George Washington would hold the office. The powers of the presidency would not have been left so loosely defined, delegate Pierce Butler of South Carolina observed, "had not many of the members cast their eyes towards General Washington as president; and shaped their ideas of the powers to be given to a president, by their opinions of his virtue." That is, the powers of the presidency were entrusted to the office not on the assumption of executive virtue, but with the knowledge of who would be the first chief executive and, by the precedents he established, would largely define the newly created office. After that, the executive would be checked by the other branches and through the electoral process.

In Article II, then, "the executive Power shall be vested in a President of the United States of America." The President plays an important role in legislation through the limited veto power (actually assigned in Article I) and the duty to recommend to Congress "such measures as he shall judge necessary and expedient." With the advice and consent of the Senate, the President appoints judges (thus shaping the judiciary) and other federal officers (thus overseeing the executive branch). Reflecting his role in directing the nation's foreign affairs, the President also (again with the advice and consent of the

Senate) appoints ambassadors and makes treaties with other nations. He also receives ambassadors from other countries and commissions all military officers of the United States.

The President is charged to "take care that the laws be faithfully executed"—a crucial responsibility necessary for the rule of law. The law to be executed is made by Congress, but when Congress creates programs and departments through its lawmaking function, those programs and departments fall operationally under the executive branch.

More generally, this means that it is the President's core responsibility to be the nation's chief executive and law-enforcement officer, who is responsible for carrying out and enforcing federal law. Every Member of Congress and every member of the federal judiciary takes an oath to "support the Constitution," but it is the President's exclusive oath, prescribed in Article II, to "faithfully execute the Office of President of the United States, and...preserve, protect and defend the Constitution of the United States."

It is important to note that the President has unique constitutional powers that do not stem from congressional authority. The President is vested directly with power in Article II of the Constitution, not by virtue of Congress's lawmaking power. Article II is a *general* grant of executive power to the President, very different from the "legislative powers, herein granted" to Congress in Article I. The President is granted all of the executive powers, except for those specifically granted to Congress (see below). This is especially the case when it comes to war and national security, for the President acts as commander in chief of the armed forces.

The office of the President is the Constitution's recognition of the basic responsibilities of government (foreign policy, national security, and the common defense) and the practical necessity that the task be directed by one person (rather than 535 Members of Congress) with adequate support and competent powers to act with the decisiveness and speed that is often required in times of crisis and conflict. The executive power is not unlimited, though, as the general grant of power is mitigated by the fact that many traditionally executive powers—to coin money, to grant letters of marque and reprisal, to raise and support armies—were given to Congress. The most significant of these limits on the executive is that Congress has the sole power to declare war. Moreover, the President has no power to enforce state laws; presidential executive power is limited to federal matters.

Often misunderstood as undemocratic, Article II also created the unique and important mechanism by which the President and Vice President are elected. In the original conception, there were no presidential campaigns, no "tickets" of candidates, and no political parties to support campaigns. Individuals were chosen (the first choice would be President, and the second choice would be Vice President) by a college of electors from each state. This was designed to encourage the selection of highly respected chief executives with nationwide credentials and with broad and general (rather than regional and narrow) appeal.

Today, the electoral college requires presidential candidates to campaign across the country and win electoral votes spread out in states (according to representation in Congress) rather than simply winning the national popular vote. In addition, while the Constitution originally allowed a President to be re-elected for an unlimited number of four-year terms, it was amended in 1952 (after Franklin Roosevelt had been elected four times) to lock in George Washington's tradition of serving only two terms.

ARTICLE III: THE JUDICIAL POWER

Article III, the shortest of the first three articles, vests the judicial power in "one supreme Court and in such inferior Courts as the Congress may from time to time ordain and establish." Justices of the Supreme Court and all federal judges are nominated by the President and confirmed by the Senate; they hold office "during good behavior" and may be impeached by Congress. By the Judiciary Act of 1789, Congress approved a Supreme Court with a chief justice and five associates (changed in 1869 to nine, where it has remained since) and created 13 district courts, three circuit courts, and the office of the Attorney General. Federal trial courts (United States District Courts) have existed in every state since 1789, and intermediate courts of appeal have existed since 1891.

There have been judges and courts throughout history, but the judiciary was not previously understood to be or to require a separate branch of government. The highest court in the British system was the House of Lords, the upper chamber of the legislature, but experience taught, and the American Founders recognized, the importance of an independent judiciary for the rule of law—the need for an impartial body to decide cases of law outside of the lawmaking and law-enforcing elements of government.

"The dignity and stability of government in all its branches, the morals of the people, and every blessing of society depend so much upon an upright and skillful administration of justice," John Adams wrote in *Thoughts on Government*, "that the judicial power ought to be distinct from both the legislative and executive, and independent upon both, that so it may be a check upon both, as both should be checks upon that." An independent judiciary is vitally important—not to *make* the law but to *uphold* and *apply* it fairly and impartially in all cases.

Federal judges are vested with *all* of the judicial power and *only* the judicial power, which is quintessentially the power (and the judiciary's core function) to decide "cases and controversies" that come before the courts by the jurisdiction assigned in the Constitution or as regulated by Congress.

To understand fully the important role of the judiciary, we must look ahead to Article VI, which explains how the Constitution fits into the overall context of constitutional government in the United States. It begins by recognizing the debts that existed prior to the Constitution, which is to say that it recognizes that the United States existed before the United States Constitution. Most important, it makes the Constitution and the laws and treaties made pursuant to it the "supreme Law of the Land."

This means that the United States Constitution is the highest law in the United States and must be followed in all cases. It also means that subsequent laws passed (and treaties approved) by Congress that are consistent with the powers granted to Congress by the U.S. Constitution must be followed in all cases. On the other hand, claims based on state constitutions and state laws that conflict with the U.S. Constitution and laws must be disregarded.

Finally, Article VI bans religious tests for office—a key component of religious liberty—and instead binds all federal and state officeholders, by oath, to the Constitution (but not to ordinary laws or treaties). Legal restrictions and political obligations are important, but in the end, political actors within the constitutional order must give complete loyalty to and solemnly pledge to support the Constitution of the United States. Article VI makes sure that America's legal system—especially the federal and state courts—is defined and focused on the Constitution.

THE LAST ARTICLES

The important status of the states is evident throughout the Constitution. While there are some things that states explicitly cannot do (raise armies or coin money, for instance), their equal representation in the Senate can never be changed, even by constitutional amendment.

The states within the constitutional system are dealt with systematically in Article IV, which requires that every state give its "Full Faith and Credit" to the laws and decisions of every other state and that citizens of each state enjoy all privileges and immunities of citizenship in every other state—both of which are conducive to establishing the rule of law. It also provides for the admission of new states to the union as *states*, not *colonies*, on an equal footing with the original 13—an exceedingly important distinction that made for America's successful growth as a nation of states rather than as a colonial empire. Finally, Article IV stipulates that the United States will guarantee to each state a republican form of government and protect the states from invasion and, upon request, domestic violence.

The process for amending the Constitution is provided for in Article V. Here we see the rule-of-law concept that the Constitution is fundamental law that can be changed, thus allowing for constitutional reform and adaptation, but only by a popular decision-making process and not by ordinary legislation or judicial decree. "As the people are the only legitimate fountain of power and it is from them that the constitutional charter, under which the several branches of government hold their power, is derived," James Madison wrote in *Federalist* 49, "it seems strictly consonant to the republican theory, to recur to the same original authority" to alter the Constitution.

Neither an exclusively federal nor an exclusively state action, the amendment process is a shared responsibility of both Congress and the states representing the American people. To succeed, an amendment proposed by Congress must have the votes of two-thirds each of the House of Representatives and the Senate, or two-thirds of the states must call for a constitutional convention to propose amendments (a method that has never been employed successfully); in either case, the proposal must then be ratified by three-quarters of the states.

Changing the document too often would weaken the Constitution and cause it to be treated as an ordinary statute that can be altered by the passions of the moment. As "every appeal to the people would carry an implication of some defect in the government," Madison notes, so frequent appeals would "deprive the government of that veneration which time bestows on every thing, and without which perhaps the wisest and freest governments would not possess the requisite stability." In any event, "a constitutional road to the decision of the people ought to be marked out and kept open, for certain great and extraordinary occasions."

Article V has the double effect of affirming the Constitution's foundation in republican self-government yet making the amending task sufficiently difficult and broad-based to protect the document and elevate it to the status of higher law. This forces the development of overwhelming and long-term majorities and is intended to assure that constitutional amendments will be rare and pursued only after careful and serious consideration when it is necessary to address an issue of great national magnitude, consistent with the deeper principles of American constitutionalism, and when there is a broad-based consensus among the American people throughout the states.

Article VII provides that the Constitution shall be ratified by state conventions rather than state legislatures, again pointing to the document's legitimacy as an act of the sovereignty of the whole people. It also dates the Constitution in "the Year of our Lord" 1787 and "of the Independence of the United States of America the twelfth," thereby locating the document in time according to the two most important dates in human history, one following the religious traditions of Western civilization and the other pointing 12 years earlier to the birth of the United States as proclaimed in the Declaration of Independence.

AUXILIARY PRECAUTIONS

"A dependence on the people is, no doubt, the primary control on the government," Madison noted in *Federalist* 51, "but experience has taught mankind the necessity of auxiliary precautions." The Founders believed that citizen virtue was crucial for the success of republican government, but they knew that passion and interest were permanent parts of human nature and could not be controlled by parchment barriers alone. Rather than relying on a predominance of virtue and civic responsibility in all cases—a dangerous assumption for constitution-makers—the Founders designed a system that would harness man's competing interests not to lower politics to questions of narrow self-interest, but to provide what they called "the defect of better motives."

The two great problems of republican government are democratic or majority tyranny on the one hand and democratic ineptitude on the other. The first was the problem of majority faction, the abuse of minority or individual rights by an "interested and overbearing" majority. The second was the problem of making a democratic form of government, which is naturally weak and divided, energetic and effective enough to defend itself and serve its purposes without becoming despotic.

So in addition to the formal provisions of the document, three important but unstated mechanisms at work in the Constitution demand our attention: the extended republic, the separation of powers, and federalism. These "auxiliary precautions" constitute improvements in the science of politics developed by the Founders and form the basis of what they considered "a republican remedy for the diseases most incident to republican government." They are crucial to the operational success of our constitutional system.

REPRESENTATION AND THE EXTENDED REPUBLIC

In the American theory of constitutional government, sovereignty exists in the people, who in turn delegate certain powers to the government. Government, in order to be legitimate, must reflect the consent of the governed. In this sense, the United States is a *popular* form of government. But popular governments can vary as to the way in which they reflect democratic opinion. Strictly speaking, a pure democracy is a system by which the people rule directly, voting on each law and policy. In a representative democracy like the United States, lawmaking is done not by the people themselves, but by individuals they have chosen to represent them in the government.

The American Founders were wary of the passions of democracy and wanted to encourage a politics of settled and thoughtful public opinion. They designed a form of popular government in which the people govern—equal rights means popular consent—but their consent is reflected through a representative process under rules and regulations set down by a written constitution, which allows for majority rule at the same time that it protects minority rights. The United States is a *representative democracy* or, better yet, a *republic*. The distinction is not unimportant.

The consequence of representation—of individual citizens being represented in government rather than ruling through direct participatory democracy—is to filter democratic opinion so that "the cool and deliberate sense of the community"

(*Federalist* 63) rules rather than "every sudden breeze of passion" (*Federalist* 71) that might come over the popular will. The effect of representation—of slowing the passions and emphasizing deliberation—is to "refine and enlarge the public views" (*Federalist* 10).

The Founders sought to correct the historic problem of majority tyranny while remaining true to the principle of popular government. Giving up on democratic liberty would be a solution worse than the problem. There was no talk of turning government over to monarchs, dictators, or other nonpopular forms of rule, but it would be just as self-defeating (not to say tyrannical) in a free society to try to make everyone have the same opinions, passions, and interests. The solution of the men who wrote the Constitution, famously laid out in *The Federalist*, was to control the political effects of these differences and thwart the formation of unjust majorities while celebrating the natural diversity inherent in human liberty.

Reversing the prevailing assumption that republican government could work only in small nation-states, the Americans argued that the key to making this view of representation work was to "extend the sphere" and "expand the orbit." That is, they argued that representation would work better in a larger and more expansive nation. As a small government is dominated more easily by a majority faction (usually based on class distinctions), increasing the size of the nation would take in a greater number and variety of opinions, including many more "fit characters" to serve in public office, making it harder for a majority to form on narrow interests. The majority that did develop in such a nation would, by necessity, encompass a wider array of opinions and represent a stronger consensus grounded in the common good.

THE SEPARATION OF POWERS

Old-fashioned tyranny was also a problem. The Founders knew—as Lord Acton later famously quipped—that power corrupts and absolute power corrupts absolutely. "The accumulation of all powers," Madison explains in *Federalist* 47, "legislative, executive, and judiciary, in the same hands, whether of one, a few, or many, and whether hereditary, self-appointed, or elective, may justly be pronounced the very definition of tyranny." Keeping the powers of government divided in distinct branches is "admitted on all hands to be essential to the preservation of liberty." Here, the Founders were following the writings of Montesquieu, who made a strong case for such a division.

But it was not enough to divide power and hope that it remained nicely confined within the written barriers of the Constitution. This was especially the case with the legislature: The "parchment barriers" of early state constitutions had proven an inadequate defense against a legislative proclivity toward "everywhere extending the sphere of its activity and drawing all power into its impetuous vortex."

It is with this proclivity in mind that the Constitution grants powers to three separate and distinct branches of government, yielding the concept of the separation of powers. Each branch has only those powers granted to it and can do only what its particular grant of power authorizes it to do.

The full meaning of the separation of powers, however, goes beyond this parchment distinction. "In framing a government which is to be administered by men over men, the great difficulty lies in this," Madison wrote in *Federalist* 51. "You must first enable the government to control the governed; and in the next place oblige it to control itself."

This meant that, in addition to performing its proper constitutional functions (lawmaking, executing and adjudicating the law), there needed to be an internal check to further limit the powers of government. Rather than create another coercive authority for that purpose (a dubious proposition to say the least), the Founders not only divided power, but also set it against itself. This separation of powers, along with the further provisions for checks and balances, creates a dynamism within the workings of government that uses the interests and incentives of those in government to enforce constitutional limits beyond their mere statement.

The Constitution creates three branches of government, and each is vested with independent powers and responsibilities. Each also has its own basis of authority and serves different terms of office. No member of one branch can at the same time serve in another branch. But their powers aren't separated completely: In order to protect themselves and guard against encroachment, each department shares overlapping powers with the others.

- Before it becomes law, congressional legislation, for instance, must be approved by the executive, who also has a check against Congress in the form of the qualified veto, which the legislature in turn can override by two-thirds votes in the House and the Senate.
- The President is commander in chief, but the House has the power to declare war, and it is up to Congress to fund executive activities, including war-making.
- Treaties and judicial appointments are made by the executive but only with the advice and consent of the Senate.
- The Supreme Court can strike down executive or legislative actions that come up in cases before it as unconstitutional, but Congress has the power to re-enact or modify

overturned laws, strip the court's jurisdiction in many cases, and impeach federal judges.

The solution is found in structuring government such that "its several constituent parts may, by their mutual relations, be the means of keeping each other in their proper places," as Madison explained in *Federalist* 51. In other words, government is structured so that each branch has an interest in keeping an eye on the others, checking powers while jealously protecting its own. By giving each department an incentive to check the other—with overlapping functions and contending ambitions—the Founders devised a system that recognized and took advantage of man's natural political motivations both to use power for the common good and to keep power within constitutional boundaries. Or, as Madison put it, the "interest of the man [becomes] connected with the constitutional rights of the place."

The separation of powers and the introduction of legislative balances and checks, according to Hamilton in *Federalist* 9, are "means, and powerful means, by which the excellencies of republican government may be retained and its imperfections lessened or avoided." They discourage the concentration of power and frustrate tyranny. At the same time, they require the branches of government to collaborate and cooperate in doing their work, limiting conflict and strengthening consensus. These means also have the powerful effect of focusing individual actors on protecting their constitutional powers and carrying out their constitutional duties and functions, and that fact transforms the separation of powers from a mere negative concept to a positive and important contributor to limited government and constitutional fidelity.[13]

---

[13] See "What Separation of Powers Means for Constitutional Government," Heritage Foundation *First Principles Essay* No. 17, December 17, 2007, by Charles R. Kesler.

Jefferson called the "republican form and principles of our Constitution" and "the salutary distribution of powers" in the Constitution the "two sheet anchors of our union." "If driven from either," he predicted, "we shall be in danger of foundering."

FEDERALISM: A NATION OF STATES

While everyone knows that this is a nation of states, few seem to think that this division is more than a quirk of history. Yet federalism is a crucial component of our system of government and part of the very infrastructure that makes our political liberty possible.

At the Constitutional Convention, despite a clear recognition of the need for additional national authority in the wake of the Articles of Confederation, there was great concern that an overreaction might produce an all-powerful national government. While they harbored no doctrinaire aversion to government as such, the Founders remained distrustful of government, especially a centralized national government that resembled the British rule against which they had revolted.

The solution was a unique American innovation: a *federal* government with strong but limited national powers that respected and protected the vitality of states. Half a century later, Alexis de Tocqueville would celebrate democracy in America as precisely the result of the political life supported and encouraged by this decentralized structure.[14]

Keep in mind that the United States Constitution is but one aspect of constitutional government in the United States. There are 50 state governments, each with its own constitution,

---

[14.]   For a brief history and defense of federalism, see *Why States? The Challenge of Federalism* (Washington: The Heritage Foundation, 2007), by Eugene W. Hickok.

and they are key components of our "compound republic." Although national powers were clearly enhanced by the Constitution, the federal government was to exercise only delegated powers, the remainder being reserved to the people or the states as defined in their constitutions. The federal government was not supposed to hold all, or even most, power.

The distinction between national and state government is inherent throughout the Constitution. The government created by the Constitution, Madison explains in *Federalist* 39, is "partly national and partly federal." The House of Representatives is elected directly by the people, but to give states more leverage within the national government, equal state representation in the Senate was blended into the national legislature (and permanently guaranteed in Article V). The executive is the most national of the branches, yet the electoral college process by which the President is elected is based on states.

It is striking that in this powerful national government, there is not a single official chosen by a national constituency. The process by which the Constitution is amended is ultimately based on state approval. The document was ratified by the states.

To the extent that the United States government acts on individuals, it is national, but in the extent of its powers, it is limited to certain national functions. "Since its jurisdiction extends to certain enumerated objects only," Madison concludes, it "leaves to the several States a residuary and inviolable sovereignty over all other objects." Here is how Madison described this in *Federalist* 45:

> The powers delegated by the proposed Constitution to the federal government are few and defined. Those which are to remain in the State governments are numerous and indefinite. The former will be exercised principally on external

objects, as war, peace, negotiation, and foreign commerce; with which last the power of taxation will, for the most part, be connected. The powers reserved to the several states will extend to all the objects which, in the ordinary course of affairs, concern the lives, liberties, and properties of the people, and the internal order, improvement and prosperity of the States.

In the same way that the separation of powers works *within* the federal and state constitutions, federalism is the basic operational structure of American constitutional government as a whole and provides the process by which the two levels of government check each other. "In the compound republic of America, the power surrendered by the people is first divided between two distinct governments, and then the portion allotted to each subdivided among distinct and separate departments," wrote Madison in *Federalist* 51. "The different governments will control each other; at the same time that each will be controlled by itself."

"This balance between the National and State governments ought to be dwelt on with peculiar attention, as it is of the utmost importance," Hamilton argued at the New York state ratifying convention. "It forms a double security to the people. If one encroaches on their rights they will find a powerful protection in the other. Indeed, they will both be prevented from overpassing their constitutional limits by a certain rivalship, which will ever subsist between them."

Although federalism was a practical invention of the Constitutional Convention, the idea of maintaining strong state governments was nothing new. The general notion that political authority and decision-making should be kept as decentralized and close to home as possible was a well-established theme of the Anti-Federalists. The view of those who doubted the political efficacy of the new Constitution was that good popular government depended as much as, if not more than, upon a political community that would promote civic or public virtue as it did on a set of institutional devices designed to check the selfish impulses of the majority.

But the structure of federalism is not only an "auxiliary precaution." By keeping authority and functions divided between two levels of government, federalism recognizes legitimate national power at the same time that it protects a sphere of state autonomy and local self-government.

JUDICIAL REVIEW

As with the auxiliary precautions, the power of federal courts to declare laws unconstitutional is not stipulated in the Constitution. While it is sometimes disputed, "judicial review" is a fundamental component of judicial power and was clearly understood to be logically implicit in the judicial function as judges consider individual cases or disputes, since a party may claim that an ordinary law and the Constitution are in conflict in the particular case before them. "The Constitution ought to be the standard of construction for the laws, and that wherever there is an evident opposition, the laws ought to give place to the Constitution," wrote Hamilton in *Federalist* 81. "But this doctrine is not deducible from any circumstance peculiar to the plan of convention, but from the general theory of a limited Constitution."

The unprecedented judicial power to declare laws "unconstitutional" is a logical consequence of having a supreme written Constitution that divides government into separate and coequal branches. The case for judicial review is made by Alexander Hamilton in *Federalist* 78:

> The interpretation of the laws is the proper and peculiar province of the courts. A constitution is, in fact, and must be regarded by the judges, as a fundamental law. It therefore belongs to them to ascertain its meaning, as well as the meaning of any particular act proceeding from the legislative body. If there should happen to be an irreconcilable variance between the two, that which has the superior obligation and validity ought, of course, to be preferred; or, in other words, the Constitution ought to be preferred to the statute, the intention of the people to the intention of their agents.

In short, when there is a conflict between ordinary law and the Constitution in a case before them, courts are obligated to take the side of the Constitution. This is no different from saying that Congress, in considering legislation, and the President, in considering signing legislation into law, must do so only if that legislation is consistent with the Constitution.

The practice of judicial review is justified—and, importantly, controlled—by the idea of the Constitution as the fundamental law that limits government. "Limitations of this kind," concludes Hamilton, "can be preserved in practice no other way than through the medium of courts of justice, whose duty it must be to declare all acts contrary to the manifest tenor of the Constitution void. Without this, all the reservations of particular rights or privileges would amount to nothing." That is, without judicial review, constitutional limitations on government power would be virtually meaningless.

John Marshall makes the same point in *Marbury v. Madison*, the first Supreme Court case of judicial review, in 1803:

> It is emphatically the province and duty of the Judicial Department to say what the law is.

Those who apply the rule to particular cases must, of necessity, expound and interpret that rule. If two laws conflict with each other, the Courts must decide on the operation of each. So, if a law be in opposition to the Constitution, if both the law and the Constitution apply to a particular case, so that the Court must either decide that case conformably to the law, disregarding the Constitution, or conformably to the Constitution, disregarding the law, the Court must determine which of these conflicting rules governs the case. This is of the very essence of judicial duty. If, then, the Courts are to regard the Constitution, and the Constitution is superior to any ordinary act of the Legislature, the Constitution, and not such ordinary act, must govern the case to which they both apply.

It is sometimes presumed that judicial review gives the Supreme Court the final say in all constitutional matters, but this does not follow from the explanations of Hamilton or Marshall. "To consider the judges as the ultimate arbiters of all constitutional questions," as Jefferson put it in 1820, "would place us under the despotism of an oligarchy." Judicial review arises from and is confined by the need for impartial legal decisions concerning the protection of the rights of individuals in particular cases—the very reason for an independent judiciary.

But the judicial power does not extend to questions of a political nature—that is, concerning public policy and the public good. The courts have no authority to substitute their own preferences for laws enacted by lawmakers. "The province of the Court is solely to decide on the rights of individuals," Marshall wrote in the *Marbury* decision. "Questions, in their nature political or which are, by the Constitution and laws, submitted to the Executive, can never be made in this court."

Congress, not courts, has the power to make laws. Presidents, not judges, have the power to veto laws. Just as particular cases are to be judged by impartial and independent bodies, so questions that are inherently public or general can be decided only by representatives elected by the people. While the Constitution required the doctrine of judicial review to protect itself from legislative assault, the rule of law and the principles of republican government mean that in cases where there is not a clear constitutional question at issue (that is, in cases dealing with the policy preferences of elected representatives), the judiciary should defer to the lawmaking branch of government.[15]

A BILL OF RIGHTS

The Bill of Rights is a distinctive and impressive mark of our liberty. Unlike the citizens of many other countries, Americans are protected from their government in the exercise of fundamental equal rights.

Many speak of the Bill of Rights as if it were the whole Constitution, but that is not correct. These amendments to the Constitution have taken on a meaning that is very different from what was envisioned. The Constitutional Convention considered and unanimously rejected a motion to draw up such a bill of rights for the constitution that its delegates were framing. Why did they deny this added protection? For one thing, the Constitution already contained several related provisions, such as the clauses against *ex post facto* laws, religious tests, and the impairment of contracts. In creating a limited government

---

[15.] See "From Constitutional Interpretation to Judicial Activism: The Transformation of Judicial Review in America," Heritage Foundation *First Principles Essay* No. 2, March 3, 2006, by Christopher Wolfe.

by which rights were to be secured and the people left free to govern themselves, the Constitution, as Hamilton insisted, is itself a bill of rights.

The more important reason had to do with the difference between the state and federal constitutions. As states had broader reserved powers, bills of rights in state constitutions made sense: They were necessary to guard individual rights against very powerful state governments. But the federal government, because it possessed only those limited powers that were delegated to it in the Constitution, did not have the power to address basic individual rights, so there was no need for a federal bill of rights—indeed, one might be dangerous. Such a bill of rights, Hamilton argued in *Federalist* 84, "would contain various exceptions to powers which are not granted; and on this very account, would afford a colourable pretext to claim more than were granted. For why declare that things shall not be done which there is no power to do?"

Put another way, why state in a bill of rights that Congress shall make no law abridging free speech if Congress in the Constitution has no power to do so in the first place? And does forbidding the federal government in a bill of rights from acting in certain areas imply that the government has the power to act in other areas? If that were the case, as Madison earlier warned, then the government was "no longer a limited one, possessing enumerated powers, but an indefinite one, subject to particular exceptions."

Nevertheless, the lack of a bill of rights similar to those found in most state constitutions became an important rallying cry for the Anti-Federalists during the ratification debate, compelling the advocates of the Constitution to agree to add one in the first session of Congress.

When the first Congress convened in March 1789, Representative James Madison took charge of the process. Only 18 months before, as a member of the Philadelphia convention, Madison had opposed a bill of rights, but he wanted above all for the new constitution to be ratified and, if possible, have the widest possible popular support. If that meant adding a bill of rights, then Madison would draft the language himself to make sure that these early amendments did not impair the Constitution's original design.[16]

Based largely on George Mason's Declaration of Rights written for the Virginia Constitution of 1776, 17 amendments were quickly introduced. Congress adopted 12, and President Washington sent them to the states for ratification. By December 15, 1791, three-fourths of the states had ratified the 10 amendments (the first two proposed amendments, concerning the number of constituents for each representative and the compensation of Congressmen, were not ratified), now known collectively as the Bill of Rights.

The First Amendment guarantees *substantive* political rights involving religion, speech, press, assembly, and petition, recognizing certain areas that are to be free from federal government interference. Likewise, the Second Amendment guarantees an individual right to keep and bear arms. The next six amendments deal with more *procedural* political rights, mostly restraints on criminal procedure (warrants must be based on probable cause, no person shall be tried twice for the same offense or be forced to testify against himself, accused criminals have a right to a speedy and public trial and the assistance of counsel, the right to a trial by jury shall be preserved) that regulate the exercise of government's law enforcement power so that it is not arbitrary or excessive.

[16.] The story of the creation of the Bill of Rights is told in Robert A. Goldwin's *From Parchment to Power: How James Madison Used the Bill of Rights to Save the Constitution* (Washington: AEI Press, 1997).

The Bill of Rights also includes important property protections. The Second Amendment prohibits confiscation of arms, and the Third Amendment prohibits the lodging of troops in any home. The Fourth Amendment prohibits unreasonable searches and seizures of persons, homes, papers, and effects, and the Eighth Amendment prohibits excessive bail and fines, as well as cruel and unusual punishment, an additional protection of property in one's person. Most significantly, of course, the Fifth Amendment says that no person shall "be deprived of life, liberty, or property, without due process of law; nor shall private property be taken for public use, without just compensation." In this sense, the protection of property is both a substantive and a procedural right guaranteed by the Constitution.

The Ninth and Tenth Amendments briefly encapsulate the twofold theory of the Constitution: The purpose of the Constitution is to protect *rights* that stem not from the government but from the people themselves, and the *powers* of the national government are limited to those delegated to it by the people in the Constitution. They also address the confusion (which was Madison's concern) that may arise in misreading the other amendments to imply unlimited federal powers. While the Ninth Amendment notes that the listing of rights in the Constitution does not deny or disparage others retained by the people, the Tenth Amendment states explicitly that all government powers except for those specific powers that are granted by the Constitution to the federal government belong to the states or the people.

The purpose of the Bill of Rights—stated by both the Federalists and the Anti-Federalists—was to limit the federal government, not the states. This is underscored by the first words of the First Amendment: "Congress shall make no law..." John Marshall confirmed this when he wrote in *Barron v. Baltimore* (1833) that these amendments "could never have occurred to any human being, as a mode of doing that which might be effected by the state itself." Congress was not empowered to act in "the extraordinary occupation of improving the constitutions of the several states, by affording the people additional protection from the exercise of power by their own governments, in matters which concerned themselves alone."

For much of our history, the Bill of Rights played virtually no role in the Supreme Court's jurisprudence. It was only in 1925 that the court began to "incorporate" the Bill of Rights into the provisions of the Fourteenth Amendment, which had been adopted in 1868. As the Fourteenth Amendment applies to the states, this meant applying the provisions of the Bill of Rights against the states as well. This process proceeded by fits and starts over the course of the 20th century. Today, the Bill of Rights serves mainly to secure rights *against* the state governments—the exact reverse of the role these amendments were intended to play in our constitutional system.

AMENDMENTS TO THE CONSTITUTION

Although more than 5,000 bills proposing to amend the Constitution have been introduced in Congress since 1789, there have been only 17 additional amendments besides the Bill of Rights. A disputed Supreme Court decision (*Chisholm v. Georgia*) led to enactment of the Eleventh Amendment (1795), limiting the jurisdiction of the federal judiciary with regard to suits against states. The election of 1800, which was decided by the House of Representatives because of an electoral-vote tie, led to enactment of the Twelfth Amendment (1804), which provided for separate balloting for President and Vice President. The Civil War was followed by enactment of the Thirteenth, Fourteenth, and Fifteenth Amendments (ratified in 1865, 1868, and 1870, respectively), which abolished slavery;

conferred citizenship on all persons born or naturalized in the United States and established the rule that a state cannot "deprive any person of life, liberty, or property, without due process of law"; and made clear that the right of citizens to vote cannot be denied or abridged on account of race, color, or previous condition of servitude.

There were four amendments during the Progressive era, at the beginning of the 20th century. The Sixteenth Amendment (1913) gave Congress the power to levy taxes on incomes, from any source, without apportionment among the several states, and so was born the modern income tax. The Seventeenth Amendment (1913) provided for the direct election of Senators by popular vote, a devastating defeat for federalism. The Eighteenth Amendment (1919), the so-called prohibition amendment, prohibited the manufacture, sale, or transportation of intoxicating liquors. (This failed experiment in social reform was repealed by the Twenty-First Amendment in 1933.) The Nineteenth Amendment (1920), completing a political movement that had started much earlier, extended to women the right to vote.

The remaining amendments have dealt with the executive and elections. The Twentieth Amendment (1933) cut in half the "lame-duck" period between presidential elections and the inauguration of the new executive; the Twenty-Second Amendment (1951), following in the wake of Franklin Roosevelt's four terms, limited Presidents to two terms (the tradition up to that point); the Twenty-Third Amendment (1961) gave the District of Columbia electors in the electoral college system; the Twenty-Fourth Amendment (1964) abolished poll taxes, which were used to deny persons the right to vote in presidential and congressional primaries and elections; and the Twenty-Fifth Amendment (1967) established the procedure (following in the wake of the Kennedy assassination) for presidential succession.

With the military draft of 18-year-old males during the Vietnam conflict, the Twenty-Sixth Amendment (1971) lowered the voting age to 18, and the most recent change was the Twenty-Seventh Amendment, which provided that any pay raise Congress votes itself would not take effect until after an intervening congressional election. It was ratified finally in 1992, 203 years after James Madison wrote and proposed it as part of the original Bill of Rights.

WHO SAYS WHAT THE CONSTITUTION MEANS?

Who, then, does have the final say as to the meaning of the Constitution? Strictly speaking, the Constitution is silent on the matter. The Supreme Court has the say in particular cases and controversies before it, and no lower-level federal or state court can reverse a Supreme Court decision, but it is not the same with the general judgments of the court. These judgments, or "holdings," are the written opinions of the justices that go beyond the particulars of the case. They are important in guiding other judges, officials. and the public as to how the Supreme Court will decide similar cases that might come before it. They track the Supreme Court's jurisprudence over time, creating stability and setting precedents for future courts to consider—a crucially important aspect of the rule of law. But the judgments of the Supreme Court beyond the decision between the parties in the immediate case or controversy are always provisional and never *final*.

In practice, either by its own reconsideration or as retiring judges are replaced by new appointees, the Supreme Court has often revised or even reversed its earlier decisions. (Over the long run, the court has reversed itself on average more than once every term.) Beyond that, Congress could withdraw the court's appellate jurisdiction or remove original jurisdiction from the lower federal courts, leaving certain issues to state courts. Ultimately, a Supreme Court decision could be overturned by a constitutional amendment, as has happened on a few occasions. It has not been unknown for Presidents to refuse to enforce the court's holdings or general judgments, the most famous example being Lincoln's refusal to uphold the *Dred Scott* decision beyond the immediate parties to the case.

That said, these last few actions, taken by institutions other than the court itself, have proven to be rare. In the overwhelming number of cases, the Supreme Court's rulings stand and take root, giving the appearance of finality. Nevertheless, it is important to recognize that the Constitution is not merely whatever the Supreme Court says it is. The decisions of the Supreme Court, no matter how benighted or controversial, never replace the Constitution.

Just as the Supreme Court is not the *final* interpreter, nor is it the *exclusive* interpreter of the Constitution. Judges, Congressmen, and Presidents all take an oath to uphold the Constitution, which means, as Madison put it, that "each must in the exercise of its functions be guided by the text of the Constitution according to its own interpretation of it." After all, it is the Constitution—and not the legislature, the executive, or the courts—that is the supreme law of the land. And just as the Supreme Court must take the side of the Constitution in interpreting the laws in cases before it (judicial review), so Congress in making laws and the President in signing and then executing laws are required—by the very nature of delegated powers in a written constitution, as well as their solemn oath of office—to do the same in the exercise of their functions. Here is how Jefferson described "coordinate branch construction" in an 1804 letter:

> [N]othing in the Constitution has given [the judiciary] a right to decide for the Executive, more than to the executive to decide for them. Both magistracies are equally independent in the sphere of action assigned to them.... [The Constitution] meant that its coordinate branches should be checks on each other. But the opinion which gives to the judges the right to decide what laws are constitutional, and what are not, not only for themselves in their own sphere of action, but for the Legislature & Executive also, in their spheres, would make the judiciary a despotic branch.

Neither the legislative nor the executive can check and balance the other branches of government—and neither can stand up to the judiciary—unless they take seriously their responsibility to act according to their interpretation of the Constitution. For the elected branches of government to turn this authority over to the courts is an abdication of both constitutional responsibility and popular consent. Lincoln put it this way in his First Inaugural, having in mind the Supreme Court's *Dred Scott* decision:

> If the policy of the Government upon vital questions, affecting the whole people, is to be irrevocably fixed by decisions of the Supreme Court, the instant they are made, in ordinary litigation between parties in personal actions, the people will have ceased to be their own rulers, having to that extent practically resigned their Government into the hands of that eminent tribunal.

Regarding the question of how to read the Constitution, there have long been certain common-sense rules for interpreting legal documents. These rules, having grown out of British constitutional thought, were well known and widely accepted at the time of the American Founding, even if they are less so today. They are ultimately rooted in principles of justice, reflecting the idea that all man-made law is based on a higher or permanent unwritten law.

"The first and governing maxim in the interpretation of a statute is to discover the meaning of those who made it," wrote James Wilson in his famed *Lectures on Law*. This is because the Constitution was adopted by a sovereign act of the people precisely for the purpose of creating a fundamental law above ordinary legislation and the political winds of the times. Joseph Story agreed in his *Commentaries on the Constitution*:

> Temporary delusions, prejudices, excitements, and objects have irresistible influence in mere questions of policy. And the policy of one age may ill suit the wishes or the policy of another. The constitution is not subject to such fluctuations. It is to have a fixed, uniform, permanent construction. It should be, so far at least as human infirmity will allow, not dependent upon the passions or parties of particular times, but the same yesterday, today, and for ever.

A proper constitutional jurisprudence, then, requires those who make, interpret, and enforce the law to be guided by the Constitution—the supreme law of the land—according to the original meaning and intent of the people who adopted it. "On every question of construction," wrote Jefferson, "we should carry ourselves back to the time when the Constitution was adopted, recollect the spirit manifested in the debates, and instead of trying what meaning may be squeezed out of the text, or invented against it, conform to the probable one in which it was passed." Such a jurisprudence is the only approach that comports with a written constitution of fundamental law based on unchanging principles of justice. "Our peculiar security is in the possession of a written Constitution," Jefferson wrote on another occasion. "Let us not make it a blank paper by construction."

While there have always been debates over the details of *what* was intended in the Constitution—for instance, between a "strict" and "loose" interpretation of its clauses—there should be no question over *whether* the original meaning of the Constitution should be the ultimate guide for constitutional interpretation. "I entirely concur in the propriety of resorting to the sense in which the Constitution was accepted and ratified by the nation," wrote James Madison. "In that sense alone it is the legitimate Constitution. And if that be not the guide in expounding it, there can be no security for a consistent and stable, more than a faithful exercise of its powers." If the Constitution is to be taken seriously, the place to start is to understand and respect its original meaning.[17]

A WORD FITLY SPOKEN

The great challenge of free government, as the Founders understood it, was to restrict and structure the powers of government in order to secure the rights articulated in the Declaration of Independence, preventing tyranny while preserving liberty. The solution was to create a strong, energetic government of limited authority, its powers enumerated in a written constitution, separated into different functions and responsibilities, and further divided between the national and state governments

---

[17.] See "How to Read the Constitution: Self-Government and the Jurisprudence of Originalism," Heritage Foundation *First Principles Essay* No. 5, May 1, 2006, by Keith E. Whittington.

in a system of federalism. The resulting framework of limited government leaves ample room for republican self-government.

A general agreement on the core principles expressed in the Declaration of Independence and the United States Constitution—equal rights grounded in a permanent human nature, constitutionalism and the rule of law, republican self-government—formed the underlying consensus of the American political tradition, underscored by the experience of American political life. Despite their various (and sometimes significant) disagreements and the eventual divisions among them that led to the establishment of the first political parties in the United States, Washington, Madison, Hamilton, Jefferson, Adams, and the other leading Founders all agreed when it came to the foundational concepts behind the American idea of liberty and constitutionalism.

This principled consensus—transcending important differences of practical application and party competition—held from the time of the Founding to the end of the 19th century, through the decline of the Federalists to the rise of the Democratic-Republicans, from the Jacksonians to the Civil War. Indeed, the one great exception proves the rule.

The Civil War of 1861–1865 represented a profound disagreement over the most basic meaning of America's foundational principles. Eleven southern slave states declared their secession from the United States and sought to form the Confederate States of America, while the remaining free states and the five border slave states remained loyal to the union under President Abraham Lincoln. Some, like Senator John C. Calhoun of South Carolina, had denied the principle of human equality and gone so far as to embrace slavery as a "positive good." Alexander Stephens, the vice president of the Confederacy, argued that slavery would be the cornerstone of their new nation. Chief Justice Roger B. Taney argued for the Supreme

Court in *Dred Scott v. Sanford* that slaves were property and "had no rights which the white man was bound to respect." Senator Stephen Douglas of Illinois hoped to solve the problem by turning to "popular sovereignty" and allowing territories and new states to decide for themselves whether to endorse slavery or not. It did not matter what they decided as long as a majority consented.

Abraham Lincoln rejected these views. He held that slavery violated the Declaration of Independence and recalled the nation to the Founders' Constitution and the principles it enshrined in order to place slavery once again on "the road to ultimate extinction."

Lincoln exemplified the older understanding of a formal constitutionalism built on the foundations of permanent principles. He once explained the relationship between the Declaration of Independence and the Constitution by reference to Proverbs 25:11: "A word fitly spoken is like apples of gold in a setting of silver." While he revered the Constitution and was a great defender of the union, he knew that the word "fitly spoken"—the apple of gold—was the assertion of principle in the Declaration of Independence. "The *Union*, and the *Constitution*, are the *picture of silver*, subsequently framed around it," Lincoln wrote. "The *picture* was made *for* the apple—*not* the apple for the picture."

Lincoln maintained that the Constitution was made to secure the principles proclaimed in the Declaration of Independence and that those principles and the Constitution, properly understood, were perfectly compatible. His great achievement, in probably the most trying epoch of our history, was to preserve our constitutional republic while restoring its dedication to the timeless principles of liberty that form the central idea of America.[18]

It was in the years after the Civil War that widespread calls for rethinking and reform led some to conclude that the original constitutional system had failed and that America needed a new way of thinking appropriate for the modern age. These "progressives" set out to create a movement that for the first time self-consciously aimed at fundamentally transforming the principles and practices of American constitutionalism.

Based on these new ideas, modern liberalism over the course of the 20th century repudiated America's core principles, holding that there are no self-evident truths but only relative values, no permanent rights but only changing rights held at the indulgence of government. As the prominent progressive historian Carl Becker put it in 1922, "To ask whether the natural rights philosophy of the Declaration of Independence is true or false, is essentially a meaningless question." By this argument, any concepts of natural right or natural law—that is, ideas of right and law grounded in a fixed or enduring nature—had to be rejected in favor of the constant evolution of man, politics, and society. Under the progressive theory, rights emerge from a government that constantly creates and redefines those rights—*ex nihilo* by judicial decree or *de facto* by Congress in the form of entitlements—to keep up with the times.

Today, we need to re-establish the proper understanding of rights in the American political tradition—the principle that each person equally possesses the unalienable rights with which he or she is endowed according to "the Laws of Nature and of Nature's God." Political thought in the past half-century has led to a serious re-evaluation of the Founders' conception of natural rights and natural law, giving rise to an extensive

---

18. The classic work on Lincoln's political thought is *Crisis of the House Divided: An Interpretation of the Issues in the Lincoln–Douglas Debates* (Chicago: University of Chicago Pres, 1959) and its companion volume, *A New Birth of Freedom: Abraham Lincoln and the Coming of the Civil War* (Lanham, Md.: Rowman & Littlefield, 2000), both by Harry V. Jaffa.

scholarship which needs to become more broadly influential, legitimating and bolstering what most Americans believe to be the case.

Likewise, the Constitution's focus on controlling and restricting government power and moderating democratic opinion was seen by the Progressives as not only misguided, but also a serious barrier to the activist government they thought necessary for progressive reforms. Their aim was to make the Constitution flexible and pliable, and thus capable of growth and adaptation in changing times. The original Constitution was to be replaced by the idea of a "living" Constitution that would update (and uproot) the old system of individual rights and limited government in favor of evolving rights and an activist (and unlimited) federal government. The Constitution is a "living" document that endlessly evolves and grows with the time.[19]

While not fully comprehended, the "living" Constitution concept is widely accepted today. As a result, it is generally supposed that judges have the final say concerning every constitutional question, giving modern government wide latitude and significant cover for its unlimited activities. These arguments need to be challenged and overcome in the public view, both as a matter of historical accuracy and as a necessary condition for reinvigorating limited government, constitutionalism, and the rule of law. By allowing the Constitution to be treated as a malleable document, we should not be surprised that the "living" Constitution has deadened the political mind of many Americans.

[19.] See "The Birth of the Administrative State: Where It Came From and What It Means for Limited Government," Heritage Foundation *First Principles Essay* No. 16, November 20, 2007, by Ronald J. Pestritto, as well as "Progressivism and the New Science of Jurisprudence," Heritage Foundation *First Principles Essay* No. 24, February 24, 2009, by Bradley C. S. Watson.

The Declaration of Independence, Jefferson wrote, was "neither aiming at originality of principle or sentiment, nor yet copied from any particular and previous writing, it was intended to be an expression of the American mind." Our aim must be a clear expression and forthright defense of America's principles in the public square so that they become once again an expression of the American mind.

Despite constant criticism and scorn by academic elites, political leaders, and the popular media, most Americans still believe in the uniqueness of this country and respect the noble ideas put forth by the American Founders. We must give voice to all those who have not given up on their country's experiment in self-government, have not concluded that the cause of liberty and limited constitutional government is lost or that America's decline is inevitable. The goal must be to restore the principles of the American Founding as the defining public philosophy of our nation.

We don't need to remake America or discover new and untested principles. We must look to the principles of the American Founding not as a matter of historical curiosity but as a source of assurance and direction for our times. The change we need is not the rejection of America's principles but a great renewal of these permanent truths about man, politics, and liberty—the foundational principles and constitutional wisdom that are the true roots of our country's greatness.

To this day, the Declaration of Independence and the United States Constitution serve not only as powerful beacons to all who strive for liberty and seek to vindicate the principles of self-government, but also as a warning to tyrants and despots everywhere. They are the highest achievements of our political tradition and, it is fair to say, the greatest statements of human liberty ever written. Taken together, these great documents represent the liberating principles that America seeks to conserve for itself and proclaim to the world.

It is not the affirmation of a peculiar set of antiquated claims that ties us to America as much as it is our common recognition of transcendent truths that bind us all together and across time to the patriots of 1776 and the Framers of 1787. Only with this sure foundation can we go forward as a nation, addressing the great policy questions before us and continuing to secure the blessings of liberty to ourselves and our posterity.

THE DECLARATION OF INDEPENDENCE IN CONGRESS, JULY 4, 1776.
THE UNANIMOUS DECLARATION OF THE THIRTEEN UNITED STATES OF AMERICA,

When in the Course of human events, it becomes necessary for one people to dissolve the political bands which have connected them with another, and to assume among the powers of the earth, the separate and equal station to which the Laws of Nature and of Nature's God entitle them, a decent respect to the opinions of mankind requires that they should declare the causes which impel them to the separation.

We hold these truths to be self-evident, that all men are created equal, that they are endowed by their Creator with certain unalienable Rights, that among these are Life, Liberty and the pursuit of Happiness.— That to secure these rights, Governments are instituted among Men, deriving their just powers from the consent of the governed,—That whenever any Form of Government becomes destructive of these ends, it is the Right of the People to alter or to abolish it, and to institute new Government, laying its foundation on such principles and organizing its powers in such form, as to them shall seem most likely to effect their Safety and Happiness. Prudence, indeed, will dictate that Governments long established should not be changed for light and transient causes; and accordingly all experience hath shewn, that mankind are more disposed to suffer, while evils are sufferable, than to right themselves by abolishing the forms to which they are accustomed. But when a long train of abuses and usurpations, pursuing invariably the same Object evinces a design to reduce them under absolute Despotism, it is their right, it is their duty, to throw off such Government, and to provide new Guards for their future security.—Such has been the patient sufferance of these Colonies; and such is now the necessity which constrains them to alter their former Systems of Government. The history of the present King of Great Britain is a history of repeated injuries and usurpations, all having in direct object the establishment of an absolute Tyranny over these States. To prove this, let Facts be submitted to a candid world.

He has refused his Assent to Laws, the most wholesome and necessary for the public good.

He has forbidden his Governors to pass Laws of immediate and pressing importance, unless suspended in their operation till his Assent should be obtained; and when so suspended, he has utterly neglected to attend to them.

He has refused to pass other Laws for the accommodation of large districts of people, unless those people would relinquish the right of Representation in the Legislature, a right inestimable to them and formidable to tyrants only.

He has called together legislative bodies at places unusual, uncomfortable, and distant from the depository of their public Records, for the sole purpose of fatiguing them into compliance with his measures.

He has dissolved Representative Houses repeatedly, for opposing with manly firmness his invasions on the rights of the people.

He has refused for a long time, after such dissolutions, to cause others to be elected; whereby the Legislative powers, incapable of Annihilation, have returned to the People at large for their exercise; the State remaining in the mean time exposed to all the dangers of invasion from without, and convulsions within.

He has endeavoured to prevent the population of these States; for that purpose obstructing the Laws for Naturalization of Foreigners; refusing to pass others to encourage their migrations hither, and raising the conditions of new Appropriations of Lands.

He has obstructed the Administration of Justice, by refusing his Assent to Laws for establishing Judiciary powers.

He has made Judges dependent on his Will alone, for the tenure of their offices, and the amount and payment of their salaries.

He has erected a multitude of New Offices, and sent hither swarms of Officers to harrass our people, and eat out their substance.

He has kept among us, in times of peace, Standing Armies without the Consent of our legislatures.

He has affected to render the Military independent of and superior to the Civil power.

He has combined with others to subject us to a jurisdiction foreign to our constitution, and unacknowledged by our laws; giving his Assent to their Acts of pretended Legislation:

For Quartering large bodies of armed troops among us:

For protecting them, by a mock Trial, from punishment for any Murders which they should commit on the Inhabitants of these States:

For cutting off our Trade with all parts of the world:

For imposing Taxes on us without our Consent:

For depriving us in many cases, of the benefits of Trial by Jury:

For transporting us beyond Seas to be tried for pretended offences:

For abolishing the free System of English Laws in a neighbouring Province, establishing therein an Arbitrary government, and enlarging its Boundaries so as to render it at once an example and fit instrument for introducing the same absolute rule into these Colonies:

For taking away our Charters, abolishing our most valuable Laws, and altering fundamentally the Forms of our Governments:

For suspending our own Legislatures, and declaring themselves invested with power to legislate for us in all cases whatsoever.

He has abdicated Government here, by declaring us out of his Protection and waging War against us.

He has plundered our seas, ravaged our Coasts, burnt our towns, and destroyed the lives of our people.

He is at this time transporting large Armies of foreign Mercenaries to compleat the works of death, desolation and tyranny, already begun with circumstances of Cruelty & perfidy scarcely paralleled in the most barbarous ages, and totally unworthy the Head of a civilized nation.

He has constrained our fellow Citizens taken Captive on the high Seas to bear Arms against their Country, to become the executioners of their friends and Brethren, or to fall themselves by their Hands.

He has excited domestic insurrections amongst us, and has endeavoured to bring on the inhabitants of our frontiers, the merciless Indian Savages, whose known rule of warfare, is an undistinguished destruction of all ages, sexes and conditions.

In every stage of these Oppressions We have Petitioned for Redress in the most humble terms: Our repeated Petitions have been answered only by repeated injury. A Prince whose character is thus marked by every act which may define a Tyrant, is unfit to be the ruler of a free people.

Nor have We been wanting in attentions to our Brittish brethren. We have warned them from time to time of attempts by their legislature to extend an unwarrantable jurisdiction over us. We have reminded them of the circumstances of our emigration and settlement here. We have appealed to their native justice and magnanimity, and we have conjured them by the ties of our common kindred to disavow these usurpations, which, would inevitably interrupt our connections and correspondence. They too have been deaf to the voice of justice and of consanguinity. We must, therefore, acquiesce in the necessity, which denounces our Separation, and hold them, as we hold the rest of mankind, Enemies in War, in Peace Friends.

We, therefore, the Representatives of the united States of America, in General Congress, Assembled, appealing to the Supreme Judge of the world for the rectitude of our intentions, do, in the Name, and by Authority of the good People of these Colonies, solemnly publish and declare, That these United Colonies are, and of Right ought to be Free and Independent States; that they are Absolved from all Allegiance to the British Crown, and that all political connection between them and the State of Great Britain, is and ought to be totally dissolved; and that as Free and Independent States, they have full Power to levy War, conclude Peace, contract Alliances, establish Commerce, and to do all other Acts and Things which Independent States may of right do. And for the support of this Declaration, with a firm reliance on the protection of divine Providence, we mutually pledge to each other our Lives, our Fortunes and our sacred Honor.

Connecticut Samuel Huntington
Roger Sherman
William Williams
Oliver Wolcott

Delaware Thomas McKean
George Read
Caesar Rodney

Georgia	Button Gwinnett
	Lyman Hall
	George Walton
Maryland	Charles Carroll of Carrollton
	Samuel Chase
	William Paca
	Thomas Stone
Massachusetts	John Adams
	Samuel Adams
	Elbridge Gerry
	John Hancock
	Robert Treat Paine
New Hampshire	Josiah Bartlett
	Matthew Thornton
	William Whipple
New Jersey	Abraham Clark
	John Hart
	Francis Hopkinson
	Richard Stockton
	John Witherspoon
New York	William Floyd
	Francis Lewis
	Philip Livingston
	Lewis Morris
North Carolina	Joseph Hewes
	William Hooper
	John Penn

Pennsylvania   George Clymer
Benjamin Franklin
Robert Morris
John Morton
George Ross
Benjamin Rush
James Smith
George Taylor
James Wilson

Rhode Island   William Ellery
Stephen Hopkins

South Carolina   Thomas Heyward, Jr.
Thomas Lynch, Jr.
Arthur Middleton
Edward Rutledge

Virginia   Carter Braxton
Benjamin Harrison
Thomas Jefferson
Francis Lightfoot Lee
Richard Henry Lee
Thomas Nelson, Jr.
George Wythe

THE CONSTITUTION
OF THE UNITED STATES

WE THE PEOPLE of the United States, in Order to form a more perfect Union, establish Justice, insure domestic Tranquility, provide for the common defence, promote the general Welfare, and secure the Blessings of Liberty to ourselves and our Posterity, do ordain and establish this Constitution for the United States of America.

Article. I.

Section. I. All legislative Powers herein granted shall be vested in a Congress of the United States, which shall consist of a Senate and House of Representatives.

Section. 2. The House of Representatives shall be composed of Members chosen every second Year by the People of the several States, and the Electors in each State shall have the Qualifications requisite for Electors of the most numerous Branch of the State Legislature.

No Person shall be a Representative who shall not have attained to the Age of twenty five Years, and been seven Years a Citizen of the United States, and who shall not, when elected, be an Inhabitant of that State in which he shall be chosen.

[Representatives and direct Taxes shall be apportioned among the several States which may be included within this Union, according to their respective Numbers, which shall be determined by adding to the whole Number of free Persons, including those bound to Service for a Term of Years, and excluding Indians not taxed, three fifths of all other Persons.][1] The actual Enumeration shall be made within three Years after the first Meeting of the Congress of the United States, and

---

[1.] Changed by section 2 of the Fourteenth Amendment.

within every subsequent Term of ten Years, in such Manner as they shall by Law direct. The Number of Representatives shall not exceed one for every thirty Thousand, but each State shall have at Least one Representative; and until such enumeration shall be made, the State of New Hampshire shall be entitled to chuse three, Massachusetts eight, Rhode-Island and Providence Plantations one, Connecticut five, New-York six, New Jersey four, Pennsylvania eight, Delaware one, Maryland six, Virginia ten, North Carolina five, South Carolina five, and Georgia three.

When vacancies happen in the Representation from any State, the Executive Authority thereof shall issue Writs of Election to fill such Vacancies.

The House of Representatives shall chuse their Speaker and other Officers; and shall have the sole Power of Impeachment.

Section. 3. The Senate of the United States shall be composed of two Senators from each State, [chosen by the Legislature][2] thereof for six Years; and each Senator shall have one Vote.

Immediately after they shall be assembled in Consequence of the first Election, they shall be divided as equally as may be into three Classes. The Seats of the Senators of the first Class shall be vacated at the Expiration of the second Year, of the second Class at the Expiration of the fourth Year, and of the third Class at the Expiration of the sixth Year, so that one third may be chosen every second Year; [and if Vacancies happen by Resignation, or otherwise, during the Recess of the Legislature of any State, the Executive thereof may make temporary Appointments until the next Meeting of the Legislature, which shall then fill such Vacancies][3].

[2.] Changed by the Seventeenth Amendment.
[3.] Changed by the Seventeenth Amendment.

No Person shall be a Senator who shall not have attained to the Age of thirty Years, and been nine Years a Citizen of the United States, and who shall not, when elected, be an Inhabitant of that State for which he shall be chosen.

The Vice President of the United States shall be President of the Senate, but shall have no Vote, unless they be equally divided.

The Senate shall chuse their other Officers, and also a President pro tempore, in the Absence of the Vice President, or when he shall exercise the Office of President of the United States.

The Senate shall have the sole Power to try all Impeachments. When sitting for that Purpose, they shall be on Oath or Affirmation. When the President of the United States is tried, the Chief Justice shall preside: And no Person shall be convicted without the Concurrence of two thirds of the Members present.

Judgment in Cases of Impeachment shall not extend further than to removal from Office, and disqualification to hold and enjoy any Office of honor, Trust or Profit under the United States: but the Party convicted shall nevertheless be liable and subject to Indictment, Trial, Judgment and Punishment, according to Law.

Section. 4. The Times, Places and Manner of holding Elections for Senators and Representatives, shall be prescribed in each State by the Legislature thereof; but the Congress may at any time by Law make or alter such Regulations, except as to the Places of chusing Senators.

The Congress shall assemble at least once in every Year, and such Meeting shall [be on the first Monday in December,][4] unless they shall by Law appoint a different Day.

---

[4]   Changed by section 2 of the Twentieth Amendment.

Section. 5. Each House shall be the Judge of the Elections, Returns and Qualifications of its own Members, and a Majority of each shall constitute a Quorum to do Business; but a smaller Number may adjourn from day to day, and may be authorized to compel the Attendance of absent Members, in such Manner, and under such Penalties as each House may provide.

Each House may determine the Rules of its Proceedings, punish its Members for disorderly Behaviour, and, with the Concurrence of two thirds, expel a Member.

Each House shall keep a Journal of its Proceedings, and from time to time publish the same, excepting such Parts as may in their Judgment require Secrecy; and the Yeas and Nays of the Members of either House on any question shall, at the Desire of one fifth of those Present, be entered on the Journal.

Neither House, during the Session of Congress, shall, without the Consent of the other, adjourn for more than three days, nor to any other Place than that in which the two Houses shall be sitting.

Section. 6. The Senators and Representatives shall receive a Compensation for their Services, to be ascertained by Law, and paid out of the Treasury of the United States. They shall in all Cases, except Treason, Felony and Breach of the Peace, be privileged from Arrest during their Attendance at the Session of their respective Houses, and in going to and returning from the same; and for any Speech or Debate in either House, they shall not be questioned in any other Place.

No Senator or Representative shall, during the Time for which he was elected, be appointed to any civil Office under the Authority of the United States, which shall have been created, or the Emoluments whereof shall have been encreased during such time; and no Person holding any Office under the United

States, shall be a Member of either House during his Continuance in Office.

Section. 7. All Bills for raising Revenue shall originate in the House of Representatives; but the Senate may propose or concur with Amendments as on other Bills.

Every Bill which shall have passed the House of Representatives and the Senate, shall, before it become a Law, be presented to the President of the United States: If he approve he shall sign it, but if not he shall return it, with his Objections to that House in which it shall have originated, who shall enter the Objections at large on their Journal, and proceed to reconsider it. If after such Reconsideration two thirds of that House shall agree to pass the Bill, it shall be sent, together with the Objections, to the other House, by which it shall likewise be reconsidered, and if approved by two thirds of that House, it shall become a Law. But in all such Cases the Votes of both Houses shall be determined by yeas and Nays, and the Names of the Persons voting for and against the Bill shall be entered on the Journal of each House respectively. If any Bill shall not be returned by the President within ten Days (Sundays excepted) after it shall have been presented to him, the Same shall be a Law, in like Manner as if he had signed it, unless the Congress by their Adjournment prevent its Return, in which Case it shall not be a Law.

Every Order, Resolution, or Vote to which the Concurrence of the Senate and House of Representatives may be necessary (except on a question of Adjournment) shall be presented to the President of the United States; and before the Same shall take Effect, shall be approved by him, or being disapproved by him, shall be repassed by two thirds of the Senate and House of Representatives, according to the Rules and Limitations prescribed in the Case of a Bill.

Section. 8. The Congress shall have Power To lay and collect Taxes, Duties, Imposts and Excises, to pay the Debts and provide for the common Defence and general Welfare of the United States; but all Duties, Imposts and Excises shall be uniform throughout the United States;

To borrow Money on the credit of the United States;

To regulate Commerce with foreign Nations, and among the several States, and with the Indian Tribes;

To establish an uniform Rule of Naturalization, and uniform Laws on the subject of Bankruptcies throughout the United States;

To coin Money, regulate the Value thereof, and of foreign Coin, and fix the Standard of Weights and Measures;

To provide for the Punishment of counterfeiting the Securities and current Coin of the United States;

To establish Post Offices and post Roads;

To promote the Progress of Science and useful Arts, by securing for limited Times to Authors and Inventors the exclusive Right to their respective Writings and Discoveries;

To constitute Tribunals inferior to the supreme Court;

To define and punish Piracies and Felonies committed on the high Seas, and Offences against the Law of Nations;

To declare War, grant Letters of Marque and Reprisal, and make Rules concerning Captures on Land and Water;

To raise and support Armies, but no Appropriation of Money to that Use shall be for a longer Term than two Years;

To provide and maintain a Navy;

To make Rules for the Government and Regulation of the land and naval Forces;

To provide for calling forth the Militia to execute the Laws of the Union, suppress Insurrections and repel Invasions;

To provide for organizing, arming, and disciplining, the Militia, and for governing such Part of them as may be employed in the Service of the United States, reserving to the States respectively, the Appointment of the Officers, and the Authority of training the Militia according to the discipline prescribed by Congress;

To exercise exclusive Legislation in all Cases whatsoever, over such District (not exceeding ten Miles square) as may, by Cession of particular States, and the Acceptance of Congress, become the Seat of the Government of the United States, and to exercise like Authority over all Places purchased by the Consent of the Legislature of the State in which the Same shall be, for the Erection of Forts, Magazines, Arsenals, dock-Yards, and other needful Buildings;—And

To make all Laws which shall be necessary and proper for carrying into Execution the foregoing Powers, and all other Powers vested by this Constitution in the Government of the United States, or in any Department or Officer thereof.

Section. 9. The Migration or Importation of such Persons as any of the States now existing shall think proper to admit, shall not be prohibited by the Congress prior to the Year one thousand eight hundred and eight, but a Tax or duty may be imposed on such Importation, not exceeding ten dollars for each Person.

The Privilege of the Writ of Habeas Corpus shall not be suspended, unless when in Cases of Rebellion or Invasion the public Safety may require it.

No Bill of Attainder or ex post facto Law shall be passed.

No Capitation, or other direct, Tax shall be laid, [unless in Proportion to the Census or enumeration herein before directed to be taken].[5]

No Tax or Duty shall be laid on Articles exported from any State.

---

[5] See Sixteenth Amendment.

No Preference shall be given by any Regulation of Commerce or Revenue to the Ports of one State over those of another; nor shall Vessels bound to, or from, one State, be obliged to enter, clear, or pay Duties in another.

No Money shall be drawn from the Treasury, but in Consequence of Appropriations made by Law; and a regular Statement and Account of the Receipts and Expenditures of all public Money shall be published from time to time.

No Title of Nobility shall be granted by the United States: And no Person holding any Office of Profit or Trust under them, shall, without the Consent of the Congress, accept of any present, Emolument, Office, or Title, of any kind whatever, from any King, Prince, or foreign State.

Section. 10. No State shall enter into any Treaty, Alliance, or Confederation; grant Letters of Marque and Reprisal; coin Money; emit Bills of Credit; make any Thing but gold and silver Coin a Tender in Payment of Debts; pass any Bill of Attainder, ex post facto Law, or Law impairing the Obligation of Contracts, or grant any Title of Nobility.

No State shall, without the Consent of the Congress, lay any Imposts or Duties on Imports or Exports, except what may be absolutely necessary for executing it's inspection Laws: and the net Produce of all Duties and Imposts, laid by any State on Imports or Exports, shall be for the Use of the Treasury of the United States; and all such Laws shall be subject to the Revision and Controul of the Congress.

No State shall, without the Consent of Congress, lay any Duty of Tonnage, keep Troops, or Ships of War in time of Peace, enter into any Agreement or Compact with another State, or with a foreign Power, or engage in War, unless actually invaded, or in such imminent Danger as will not admit of delay.

Article. II.

Section. I. The executive Power shall be vested in a President of the United States of America. He shall hold his Office during the Term of four Years, and, together with the Vice President, chosen for the same Term, be elected, as follows:

Each State shall appoint, in such Manner as the Legislature thereof may direct, a Number of Electors, equal to the whole Number of Senators and Representatives to which the State may be entitled in the Congress: but no Senator or Representative, or Person holding an Office of Trust or Profit under the United States, shall be appointed an Elector.

[The Electors shall meet in their respective States, and vote by Ballot for two Persons, of whom one at least shall not be an Inhabitant of the same State with themselves. And they shall make a List of all the Persons voted for, and of the Number of Votes for each; which List they shall sign and certify, and transmit sealed to the Seat of the Government of the United States, directed to the President of the Senate. The President of the Senate shall, in the Presence of the Senate and House of Representatives, open all the Certificates, and the Votes shall then be counted. The Person having the greatest Number of Votes shall be the President, if such Number be a Majority of the whole Number of Electors appointed; and if there be more than one who have such Majority, and have an equal Number of Votes, then the House of Representatives shall immediately chuse by Ballot one of them for President; and if no Person have a Majority, then from the five highest on the List the said House shall in like Manner chuse the President. But in chusing the President, the Votes shall be taken by States, the Representation from each State having one Vote; A quorum for this purpose shall consist of a Member or Members from two thirds of the States, and a Majority of all the States shall be necessary to a Choice. In every Case, after the Choice of the

President, the Person having the greatest Number of Votes of the Electors shall be the Vice President. But if there should remain two or more who have equal Votes, the Senate shall chuse from them by Ballot the Vice President.][6]

The Congress may determine the Time of chusing the Electors, and the Day on which they shall give their Votes; which Day shall be the same throughout the United States.

No Person except a natural born Citizen, or a Citizen of the United States, at the time of the Adoption of this Constitution, shall be eligible to the Office of President; neither shall any Person be eligible to that Office who shall not have attained to the Age of thirty five Years, and been fourteen Years a Resident within the United States.

[In Case of the Removal of the President from Office, or of his Death, Resignation, or Inability to discharge the Powers and Duties of the said Office, the Same shall devolve on the Vice President, and the Congress may by Law provide for the Case of Removal, Death, Resignation or Inability, both of the President and Vice President, declaring what Officer shall then act as President, and such Officer shall act accordingly, until the Disability be removed, or a President shall be elected.][7]

The President shall, at stated Times, receive for his Services, a Compensation, which shall neither be increased nor diminished during the Period for which he shall have been elected, and he shall not receive within that Period any other Emolument from the United States, or any of them.

Before he enter on the Execution of his Office, he shall take the following Oath or Affirmation:—"I do solemnly swear (or affirm) that I will faithfully execute the Office of President of the United States, and will to the best of my Ability, preserve, protect and defend the Constitution of the United States."

[6.] Changed by the Twelfth Amendment.
[7.] Changed by the Twenty-Fifth Amendment.

Section. 2. The President shall be Commander in Chief of the Army and Navy of the United States, and of the Militia of the several States, when called into the actual Service of the United States; he may require the Opinion, in writing, of the principal Officer in each of the executive Departments, upon any Subject relating to the Duties of their respective Offices, and he shall have Power to grant Reprieves and Pardons for Offences against the United States, except in Cases of Impeachment.

He shall have Power, by and with the Advice and Consent of the Senate, to make Treaties, provided two thirds of the Senators present concur; and he shall nominate, and by and with the Advice and Consent of the Senate, shall appoint Ambassadors, other public Ministers and Consuls, Judges of the supreme Court, and all other Officers of the United States, whose Appointments are not herein otherwise provided for, and which shall be established by Law: but the Congress may by Law vest the Appointment of such inferior Officers, as they think proper, in the President alone, in the Courts of Law, or in the Heads of Departments.

The President shall have Power to fill up all Vacancies that may happen during the Recess of the Senate, by granting Commissions which shall expire at the End of their next Session.

Section. 3. He shall from time to time give to the Congress Information of the State of the Union, and recommend to their Consideration such Measures as he shall judge necessary and expedient; he may, on extraordinary Occasions, convene both Houses, or either of them, and in Case of Disagreement between them, with Respect to the Time of Adjournment, he may adjourn them to such Time as he shall think proper; he shall receive Ambassadors and other public Ministers; he shall take Care that the Laws be faithfully executed, and shall Commission all the Officers of the United States.

Section. 4. The President, Vice President and all civil Officers of the United States, shall be removed from Office on Impeachment for, and Conviction of, Treason, Bribery, or other high Crimes and Misdemeanors.

Article III.

Section. I. The judicial Power of the United States shall be vested in one supreme Court, and in such inferior Courts as the Congress may from time to time ordain and establish. The Judges, both of the supreme and inferior Courts, shall hold their Offices during good Behaviour, and shall, at stated Times, receive for their Services a Compensation, which shall not be diminished during their Continuance in Office.

Section. 2. The judicial Power shall extend to all Cases, in Law and Equity, arising under this Constitution, the Laws of the United States, and Treaties made, or which shall be made, under their Authority;—to all Cases affecting Ambassadors, other public Ministers and Consuls;—to all Cases of admiralty and maritime Jurisdiction;—to Controversies to which the United States shall be a Party;—to Controversies between two or more States;— [between a State and Citizens of another State;]⁸—between Citizens of different States;—between Citizens of the same State claiming Lands under Grants of different States, [and between a State, or the Citizens thereof, and foreign States, Citizens or Subjects.]⁹

In all Cases affecting Ambassadors, other public Ministers and Consuls, and those in which a State shall be Party, the supreme Court shall have original Jurisdiction. In all the other Cases before mentioned, the supreme Court shall have appellate Jurisdiction, both as to Law and Fact, with such Exceptions, and under such Regulations as the Congress shall make.

---

8. Changed by the Eleventh Amendment.
9. Changed by the Eleventh Amendment.

The Trial of all Crimes, except in Cases of Impeachment, shall be by Jury; and such Trial shall be held in the State where the said Crimes shall have been committed; but when not committed within any State, the Trial shall be at such Place or Places as the Congress may by Law have directed.

  Section. 3. Treason against the United States, shall consist only in levying War against them, or in adhering to their Enemies, giving them Aid and Comfort. No Person shall be convicted of Treason unless on the Testimony of two Witnesses to the same overt Act, or on Confession in open Court.

The Congress shall have Power to declare the Punishment of Treason, but no Attainder of Treason shall work Corruption of Blood, or Forfeiture except during the Life of the Person attainted.

Article. IV.

Section. I. Full Faith and Credit shall be given in each State to the public Acts, Records, and judicial Proceedings of every other State. And the Congress may by general Laws prescribe the Manner in which such Acts, Records and Proceedings shall be proved, and the Effect thereof.

Section. 2. The Citizens of each State shall be entitled to all Privileges and Immunities of Citizens in the several States.

A Person charged in any State with Treason, Felony, or other Crime, who shall flee from Justice, and be found in another State, shall on Demand of the executive Authority of the State from which he fled, be delivered up, to be removed to the State having Jurisdiction of the Crime.

[No Person held to Service or Labour in one State, under the Laws thereof, escaping into another, shall, in Consequence of any Law or Regulation therein, be discharged from such

Service or Labour, but shall be delivered up on Claim of the Party to whom such Service or Labour may be due.][10]

Section. 3. New States may be admitted by the Congress into this Union; but no new State shall be formed or erected within the Jurisdiction of any other State; nor any State be formed by the Junction of two or more States, or Parts of States, without the Consent of the Legislatures of the States concerned as well as of the Congress.

The Congress shall have Power to dispose of and make all needful Rules and Regulations respecting the Territory or other Property belonging to the United States; and nothing in this Constitution shall be so construed as to Prejudice any Claims of the United States, or of any particular State.

Section. 4. The United States shall guarantee to every State in this Union a Republican Form of Government, and shall protect each of them against Invasion; and on Application of the Legislature, or of the Executive (when the Legislature cannot be convened), against domestic Violence.

Article. V.

The Congress, whenever two thirds of both Houses shall deem it necessary, shall propose Amendments to this Constitution, or, on the Application of the Legislatures of two thirds of the several States, shall call a Convention for proposing Amendments, which, in either Case, shall be valid to all Intents and Purposes, as Part of this Constitution, when ratified by the Legislatures of three fourths of the several States, or by Conventions in three fourths thereof, as the one or the other Mode of Ratification may be proposed by the Congress; Provided that no Amendment which may be made prior to the Year One thousand eight hundred and eight shall in any Manner affect the first and fourth Clauses in the Ninth Section of the first

---

10. Changed by the Thirteenth Amendment.

Article; and that no State, without its Consent, shall be deprived of its equal Suffrage in the Senate.

Article. VI.

All Debts contracted and Engagements entered into, before the Adoption of this Constitution, shall be as valid against the United States under this Constitution, as under the Confederation.

This Constitution, and the Laws of the United States which shall be made in Pursuance thereof; and all Treaties made, or which shall be made, under the Authority of the United States, shall be the supreme Law of the Land; and the Judges in every State shall be bound thereby, any Thing in the Constitution or Laws of any State to the Contrary notwithstanding.

The Senators and Representatives before mentioned, and the Members of the several State Legislatures, and all executive and judicial Officers, both of the United States and of the several States, shall be bound by Oath or Affirmation, to support this Constitution; but no religious Test shall ever be required as a Qualification to any Office or public Trust under the United States.

Article. VII.

The Ratification of the Conventions of nine States, shall be sufficient for the Establishment of this Constitution between the States so ratifying the Same.

Done in Convention by the Unanimous Consent of the States present the Seventeenth Day of September in the Year of our Lord one thousand seven hundred and Eighty seven and of the Independence of the United States of America the Twelfth In witness whereof We have hereunto subscribed our Names,

Gº. Washington
Presidt and deputy from Virginia

Delaware
Geo: Read
Gunning Bedford jun
John Dickinson
Richard Bassett
Jaco: Broom

Maryland
James McHenry
Dan of St Thos. Jenifer
Danl. Carroll

Virginia
John Blair
James Madison Jr.

North Carolina
Wm. Blount
Richd. Dobbs Spaight
Hu Williamson

South Carolina
J. Rutledge
Charles Cotesworth Pinckney
Charles Pinckney
Pierce Butler

Georgia
William Few
Abr Baldwin

New Hampshire
John Langdon
Nicholas Gilman

Massachusetts
Nathaniel Gorham
Rufus King

Connecticut	Wm. Saml. Johnson
	Roger Sherman
New York	Alexander Hamilton
New Jersey	Wil: Livingston
	David Brearley
	Wm. Paterson
	Jona: Dayton
Pennsylvania	B Franklin
	Thomas Mifflin
	Robt. Morris
	Geo. Clymer
	Thos. FitzSimons
	Jared Ingersoll
	James Wilson
	Gouv Morris

Attest William Jackson Secretary

AMENDMENTS TO THE
CONSTITUTION OF THE UNITED STATES

Amendment I[11]

Congress shall make no law respecting an establishment of religion, or prohibiting the free exercise thereof; or abridging the freedom of speech, or of the press; or the right of the people peaceably to assemble, and to petition the Government for a redress of grievances.

Amendment II

A well regulated Militia, being necessary to the security of a free State, the right of the people to keep and bear Arms, shall not be infringed.

Amendment III

No Soldier shall, in time of peace be quartered in any house, without the consent of the Owner, nor in time of war, but in a manner to be prescribed by law.

Amendment IV

The right of the people to be secure in their persons, houses, papers, and effects, against unreasonable searches and seizures, shall not be violated, and no Warrants shall issue, but upon probable cause, supported by Oath or affirmation, and particularly describing the place to be searched, and the persons or things to be seized.

Amendment V

No person shall be held to answer for a capital, or otherwise infamous crime, unless on a presentment or indictment

---

[11]   The first ten Amendments (Bill of Rights) were ratified effective December 15, 1791.

of a Grand Jury, except in cases arising in the land or naval forces, or in the Militia, when in actual service in time of War or public danger; nor shall any person be subject for the same offence to be twice put in jeopardy of life or limb; nor shall be compelled in any criminal case to be a witness against himself, nor be deprived of life, liberty, or property, without due process of law; nor shall private property be taken for public use, without just compensation.

Amendment VI

In all criminal prosecutions, the accused shall enjoy the right to a speedy and public trial, by an impartial jury of the State and district wherein the crime shall have been committed, which district shall have been previously ascertained by law, and to be informed of the nature and cause of the accusation; to be confronted with the witnesses against him; to have compulsory process for obtaining witnesses in his favor, and to have the Assistance of Counsel for his defence.

Amendment VII

In Suits at common law, where the value in controversy shall exceed twenty dollars, the right of trial by jury shall be preserved, and no fact tried by a jury, shall be otherwise reexamined in any Court of the United States, than according to the rules of the common law.

Amendment VIII

Excessive bail shall not be required, nor excessive fines imposed, nor cruel and unusual punishments inflicted.

Amendment IX

The enumeration in the Constitution, of certain rights, shall not be construed to deny or disparage others retained by the people.

Amendment X

The powers not delegated to the United States by the Constitution, nor prohibited by it to the States, are reserved to the States respectively, or to the people.

Amendment XI[12]

The Judicial power of the United States shall not be construed to extend to any suit in law or equity, commenced or prosecuted against one of the United States by Citizens of another State, or by Citizens or Subjects of any Foreign State.

Amendment XII[13]

The Electors shall meet in their respective states and vote by ballot for President and Vice-President, one of whom, at least, shall not be an inhabitant of the same state with themselves; they shall name in their ballots the person voted for as President, and in distinct ballots the person voted for as Vice-President, and they shall make distinct lists of all persons voted for as President, and of all persons voted for as Vice-President, and of the number of votes for each, which lists they shall sign and certify, and transmit sealed to the seat of the government of the United States, directed to the President of the Senate;—the President of the Senate shall, in the presence of the Senate and House of Representatives, open all the certificates and the votes shall then be counted;—The

---

[12]   The Eleventh Amendment was ratified February 7, 1795.
[13]   The Twelfth Amendment was ratified June 15, 1804.

person having the greatest number of votes for President, shall be the President, if such number be a majority of the whole number of Electors appointed; and if no person have such majority, then from the persons having the highest numbers not exceeding three on the list of those voted for as President, the House of Representatives shall choose immediately, by ballot, the President. But in choosing the President, the votes shall be taken by states, the representation from each state having one vote; a quorum for this purpose shall consist of a member or members from two-thirds of the states, and a majority of all the states shall be necessary to a choice. [And if the House of Representatives shall not choose a President whenever the right of choice shall devolve upon them, before the fourth day of March next following, then the Vice-President shall act as President, as in case of the death or other constitutional disability of the President.—][14] The person having the greatest number of votes as Vice-President, shall be the Vice-President, if such number be a majority of the whole number of Electors appointed, and if no person have a majority, then from the two highest numbers on the list, the Senate shall choose the Vice-President; a quorum for the purpose shall consist of two-thirds of the whole number of Senators, and a majority of the whole number shall be necessary to a choice. But no person constitutionally ineligible to the office of President shall be eligible to that of Vice-President of the United States.

Amendment XIII[15]

Section I. Neither slavery nor involuntary servitude, except as a punishment for crime whereof the party shall have been duly convicted, shall exist within the United States, or any place subject to their jurisdiction.

---

14. Superseded by section 3 of the Twentieth Amendment.
15. The Thirteenth Amendment was ratified December 6, 1865.

Section 2. Congress shall have power to enforce this article by appropriate legislation.

Amendment XIV[16]

Section 1. All persons born or naturalized in the United States, and subject to the jurisdiction thereof, are citizens of the United States and of the State wherein they reside. No State shall make or enforce any law which shall abridge the privileges or immunities of citizens of the United States; nor shall any State deprive any person of life, liberty, or property, without due process of law; nor deny to any person within its jurisdiction the equal protection of the laws.

Section 2. Representatives shall be apportioned among the several States according to their respective numbers, counting the whole number of persons in each State, excluding Indians not taxed. But when the right to vote at any election for the choice of electors for President and Vice-President of the United States, Representatives in Congress, the Executive and Judicial officers of a State, or the members of the Legislature thereof, is denied to any of the male inhabitants of such State, being twenty-one years of age, and citizens of the United States, or in any way abridged, except for participation in rebellion, or other crime, the basis of representation therein shall be reduced in the proportion which the number of such male citizens shall bear to the whole number of male citizens twenty-one years of age in such State.

Section 3. No person shall be a Senator or Representative in Congress, or elector of President and Vice-President, or hold any office, civil or military, under the United States, or under any State, who, having previously taken an oath, as a member of Congress, or as an officer of the United States, or as a member of any State legislature, or as an executive or

---

16. The Fourteenth Amendment was ratified July 9, 1868.

judicial officer of any State, to support the Constitution of the United States, shall have engaged in insurrection or rebellion against the same, or given aid or comfort to the enemies thereof. But Congress may by a vote of two-thirds of each House, remove such disability.

Section 4. The validity of the public debt of the United States, authorized by law, including debts incurred for payment of pensions and bounties for services in suppressing insurrection or rebellion, shall not be questioned. But neither the United States nor any State shall assume or pay any debt or obligation incurred in aid of insurrection or rebellion against the United States, or any claim for the loss or emancipation of any slave; but all such debts, obligations and claims shall be held illegal and void.

Section 5. The Congress shall have the power to enforce, by appropriate legislation, the provisions of this article.

Amendment XV[17]

Section 1. The right of citizens of the United States to vote shall not be denied or abridged by the United States or by any State on account of race, color, or previous condition of servitude—

Section 2. The Congress shall have the power to enforce this article by appropriate legislation.

Amendment XVI[18]

The Congress shall have power to lay and collect taxes on incomes, from whatever source derived, without apportionment among the several States, and without regard to any census or enumeration.

---

[17] The Fifteenth Amendment was ratified February 3, 1870.
[18] The Sixteenth Amendment was ratified February 3, 1913.

Amendment XVII[19]

The Senate of the United States shall be composed of two Senators from each State, elected by the people thereof, for six years; and each Senator shall have one vote. The electors in each State shall have the qualifications requisite for electors of the most numerous branch of the State legislatures.

When vacancies happen in the representation of any State in the Senate, the executive authority of such State shall issue writs of election to fill such vacancies: *Provided*, That the legislature of any State may empower the executive thereof to make temporary appointments until the people fill the vacancies by election as the legislature may direct.

This amendment shall not be so construed as to affect the election or term of any Senator chosen before it becomes valid as part of the Constitution.

Amendment XVIII[20]

Section 1. After one year from the ratification of this article the manufacture, sale, or transportation of intoxicating liquors within, the importation thereof into, or the exportation thereof from the United States and all territory subject to the jurisdiction thereof for beverage purposes is hereby prohibited.

Section 2. The Congress and the several States shall have concurrent power to enforce this article by appropriate legislation.

Section 3. This article shall be inoperative unless it shall have been ratified as an amendment to the Constitution by the legislatures of the several States, as provided in the Constitution, within seven years from the date of the submission hereof to the States by the Congress.

---

[19] The Seventeenth Amendment was ratified April 8, 1913.
[20] The Eighteenth Amendment was ratified January 16, 1919. It was repealed by the Twenty-First Amendment December 5, 1933.

Amendment XIX[21]

The right of citizens of the United States to vote shall not be denied or abridged by the United States or by any State on account of sex.

Congress shall have power to enforce this article by appropriate legislation.

Amendment XX[22]

Section 1. The terms of the President and the Vice President shall end at noon on the 20th day of January, and the terms of Senators and Representatives at noon on the 3d day of January, of the years in which such terms would have ended if this article had not been ratified; and the terms of their successors shall then begin.

Section 2. The Congress shall assemble at least once in every year, and such meeting shall begin at noon on the 3d day of January, unless they shall by law appoint a different day.

Section 3. If, at the time fixed for the beginning of the term of the President, the President elect shall have died, the Vice President elect shall become President. If a President shall not have been chosen before the time fixed for the beginning of his term, or if the President elect shall have failed to qualify, then the Vice President elect shall act as President until a President shall have qualified; and the Congress may by law provide for the case wherein neither a President elect nor a Vice President shall have qualified, declaring who shall then act as President, or the manner in which one who is to act shall be selected, and such person shall act accordingly until a President or Vice President shall have qualified.

---

21. The Nineteenth Amendment was ratified August 18, 1920.
22. The Twentieth Amendment was ratified January 23, 1933.

Section 4. The Congress may by law provide for the case of the death of any of the persons from whom the House of Representatives may choose a President whenever the right of choice shall have devolved upon them, and for the case of the death of any of the persons from whom the Senate may choose a Vice President whenever the right of choice shall have devolved upon them.

Section 5. Sections 1 and 2 shall take effect on the 15th day of October following the ratification of this article.

Section 6. This article shall be inoperative unless it shall have been ratified as an amendment to the Constitution by the legislatures of three-fourths of the several States within seven years from the date of its submission.

Amendment XXI[23]

Section 1. The eighteenth article of amendment to the Constitution of the United States is hereby repealed.

Section 2. The transportation or importation into any State, Territory, or Possession of the United States for delivery or use therein of intoxicating liquors, in violation of the laws thereof, is hereby prohibited.

Section 3. This article shall be inoperative unless it shall have been ratified as an amendment to the Constitution by conventions in the several States, as provided in the Constitution, within seven years from the date of the submission hereof to the States by the Congress.

Amendment XXII[24]

Section 1. No person shall be elected to the office of the President more than twice, and no person who has held

---

[23.] The Twenty-First Amendment was ratified December 5, 1933.

[24.] The Twenty-Second Amendment was ratified February 27, 1951.

the office of President, or acted as President, for more than two years of a term to which some other person was elected President shall be elected to the office of President more than once. But this Article shall not apply to any person holding the office of President when this Article was proposed by Congress, and shall not prevent any person who may be holding the office of President, or acting as President, during the term within which this Article becomes operative from holding the office of President or acting as President during the remainder of such term.

Section 2. This article shall be inoperative unless it shall have been ratified as an amendment to the Constitution by the legislatures of three-fourths of the several States within seven years from the date of its submission to the States by the Congress.

Amendment XXIII[25]

Section 1. The District constituting the seat of Government of the United States shall appoint in such manner as Congress may direct:

A number of electors of President and Vice President equal to the whole number of Senators and Representatives in Congress to which the District would be entitled if it were a State, but in no event more than the least populous State; they shall be in addition to those appointed by the States, but they shall be considered, for the purposes of the election of President and Vice President, to be electors appointed by a State; and they shall meet in the District and perform such duties as provided by the twelfth article of amendment.

Section 2. The Congress shall have power to enforce this article by appropriate legislation.

---

25. The Twenty-Third Amendment was ratified March 29, 1961.

Amendment XXIV[26]

Section 1. The right of citizens of the United States to vote in any primary or other election for President or Vice President, for electors for President or Vice President, or for Senator or Representative in Congress, shall not be denied or abridged by the United States or any State by reason of failure to pay poll tax or other tax.

Section 2. The Congress shall have power to enforce this article by appropriate legislation.

Amendment XXV[27]

Section 1. In case of the removal of the President from office or of his death or resignation, the Vice President shall become President.

Section 2. Whenever there is a vacancy in the office of the Vice President, the President shall nominate a Vice President who shall take office upon confirmation by a majority vote of both Houses of Congress.

Section 3. Whenever the President transmits to the President pro tempore of the Senate and the Speaker of the House of Representatives his written declaration that he is unable to discharge the powers and duties of his office, and until he transmits to them a written declaration to the contrary, such powers and duties shall be discharged by the Vice President as Acting President.

Section 4. Whenever the Vice President and a majority of either the principal officers of the executive departments or of such other body as Congress may by law provide, transmit to the President pro tempore of the Senate and the Speaker of the House of Representatives their written declaration that the

---

26. The Twenty-Fourth Amendment was ratified January 23, 1964.
27. The Twenty-Fifth Amendment was ratified February 10, 1967.

President is unable to discharge the powers and duties of his office, the Vice President shall immediately assume the powers and duties of the office as Acting President.

Thereafter, when the President transmits to the President pro tempore of the Senate and the Speaker of the House of Representatives his written declaration that no inability exists, he shall resume the powers and duties of his office unless the Vice President and a majority of either the principal officers of the executive department or of such other body as Congress may by law provide, transmit within four days to the President pro tempore of the Senate and the Speaker of the House of Representatives their written declaration that the President is unable to discharge the powers and duties of his office. Thereupon Congress shall decide the issue, assembling within forty-eight hours for that purpose if not in session. If the Congress, within twenty-one days after receipt of the latter written declaration, or, if Congress is not in session, within twenty-one days after Congress is required to assemble, determines by two-thirds vote of both Houses that the President is unable to discharge the powers and duties of his office, the Vice President shall continue to discharge the same as Acting President; otherwise, the President shall resume the powers and duties of his office.

Amendment XXVI[28]

Section 1. The right of citizens of the United States, who are eighteen years of age or older, to vote shall not be denied or abridged by the United States or by any State on account of age.

Section 2. The Congress shall have power to enforce this article by appropriate legislation.

[28.] The Twenty-Sixth Amendment was ratified July 1, 1971.

Amendment XXVII[29]

No law, varying the compensation for the services of the Senators and Representatives, shall take effect, until an election of representatives shall have intervened.

[29.] The Twenty-Seventh Amendment was ratified May 7, 1992.

About the Author

*M*atthew Spalding is director of the B. Kenneth Simon Center for American Studies at The Heritage Foundation, where he also is the policy director of the First Principles Initiative. His latest book, *We Still Hold These Truths: Rediscovering Our Principles, Reclaiming Our Future* (ISI Books: 2009), is a national bestseller. He is the author or editor of several other books, including *A Sacred Union of Citizens: Washington's Farewell Address and the American Character, Patriot Sage: George Washington and the American Political Tradition,* and *The Founders' Almanac: A Practical Guide to the Notable Events, Greatest Leaders & Most Eloquent Words of the American Founding.* He is Executive Editor of *The Heritage Guide to the Constitution,* a clause-by-clause analysis of the United States Constitution. He has taught at George Mason University, the Catholic University of America, Claremont McKenna College, and Hillsdale College. Currently a fellow of the Claremont Institute for the Study of Statesmanship and Political Philosophy and an adjunct fellow of the Kirby Center for Constitutional Studies and Citizenship at Hillsdale College, Spalding lives with his family in northern Virginia.